WOOD JEWELRY

30 STYLISH PROJECTS

TERRY TAYLOR

LARK BOOKS

A Division of Sterling Publishing Co., Inc.
New York / London

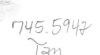

Technical Editor:
Thomas Stender

Art Director:
Dana Irwin

Design:
828:design

Cover Designer:
Celia Naranjo

Art Production Assistant:
Jeff Hamilton

Assistant Editors:
Cassie Moore and Mark Bloom

Editorial Assistance: Dawn Dillingham

Photographer:
Stewart O'Shields (Project photography);

Steve Mann, Black Box Photography
(pages 16, 18, 19, 21 bottom, 22 bottom,
23, 25, 26);

Thomas Stender (pages 9, 20, 21 top,
22 top);

Brian Hearne (wood samples, pages 10-14)

Lynne Harty (front cover, page 66 bottom)

FOR METALWORKERS,
WOODWORKERS, AND
INDEED ANYONE WHO
APPRECIATES BEAUTIFULLY
MADE JEWELRY, NO
MATTER WHAT MATERIAL
IS USED TO MAKE IT.

The Library of Congress has cataloged the hardcover edition as follows:

Taylor, Terry, 1952-
   The art of jewelry. Wood : techniques, projects, inspiration / Terry Taylor.
      p. cm.
   Includes index.
   ISBN-13: 978-1-60059-106-8 (hc-plc with jacket : alk. paper)
   ISBN-10: 1-60059-106-X (hc-plc with jacket : alk. paper)
   1. Woodwork. 2. Jewelry making. I. Title.
   TT185.T285 2008
   745.594'2--dc22

                        2007021855

10 9 8 7 6 5 4 3 2 1

Published by Lark Books, A Division of Sterling Publishing Co., Inc.
387 Park Avenue South, New York, N.Y. 10016

First Paperback Edition 2010
Text © 2007, Lark Books, A Division of Sterling Publishing Co., Inc.
Photography © 2007, Lark Books, A Division of Sterling Publishing Co., Inc.;
unless otherwise specified

Previously published as The Art of Jewelry Wood: Techniques, Projects, Inspiration

Distributed in Canada by Sterling Publishing,
c/o Canadian Manda Group, 165 Dufferin Street
Toronto, Ontario, Canada M6K 3H6

Distributed in the United Kingdom by GMC Distribution Services,
Castle Place, 166 High Street, Lewes, East Sussex, England BN7 1XU

Distributed in Australia by Capricorn Link (Australia) Pty Ltd.,
P.O. Box 704, Windsor, NSW 2756 Australia

If you have questions or comments about this book, please contact:
Lark Books
67 Broadway
Asheville, NC 28801
828-253-0467

Manufactured in China

ISBN 13: 978-1-60059-106-8 (hardcover) 978-1-60059-640-7 (paperback)

For information about custom editions, special sales, premium and corporate purchases, please contact Sterling Special Sales Department at 800-805-5489 or specialsales@sterlingpub.com.

2/10
B8+

CONTENTS

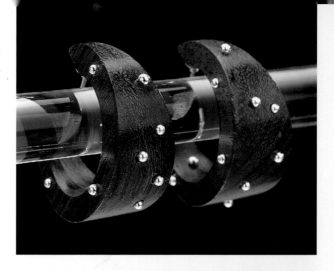

Wood Jewelry
INTRODUCTION

Wood jewelry?

You already know that wood is a versatile material: look around you. You walk on polished wood floors, lounge in maple dining chairs, burn it in your fireplace for warmth, and depend on its strength to hold up the roof over your head. And lest you forget, it's the primary material for the pages in this book. Given serious thought, you could come up with a dozen or more ways in which wood is used. But I'd wager that you wouldn't have immediately thought of wood jewelry.

Wood's versatility makes it an inspiring (if unusual) material for creating jewelry for a variety of reasons. It's easily worked with simple tools—a sharp knife is all you need, in a pinch. The sheer number of wood species offers the artist an incredible variety of color and grain patterns to choose from. Wood can be manipulated in many ways: carved, split, turned, bent, or joined. Wood surfaces can be stained, painted, gilded, or given a high polish; gouged, drilled, or even burned. And wood is light enough to wear with ease. It isn't too far-fetched to imagine early man using bits of wood for adornment, just as he employed shell, feather, fur, bone, and other natural materials. After all, wood was plentiful, beautiful, and simple to work with, even with low-tech tools such as sharpened flint or stone.

We've gathered a group of talented artisans to show you just how spectacular wood jewelry can be. They've generously shared their working techniques to inspire you and help you create your own pieces—it's easier than you might think. Carved work runs the gamut from traditional chip carved earrings (page 87) to a bold, sculptural bracelet (page 84). If your interest leans toward using found objects, a bracelet of golf tees capped with pyrite cabochons (page 39) and a mixed media bracelet of vintage wooden ruler slices will tickle your fancy. Combining metal and wood ranges from inlay earrings of silver, resin, and sawdust (page 117) to a simply carved ring with an inset silver band (page 50). Beaders will be intrigued with the necklaces on pages 30 and 32. Lovers of painted surfaces will be charmed with the works on pages 56 and 67. An intimidating technique such as wood lamination is revealed to be no more difficult than cutting, gluing, cutting, and re-gluing: it's that simple.

In addition you'll discover the wealth of different ways contemporary jewelry artists from around the world have incorporated wood into their creative vocabularies. Throughout the book you'll find a trove of images to inspire you in your own endeavors, from the elegantly sculpted necklaces of Liv Blåvarp (page 131) to the carved and painted brooches by Catherine Truman (page 24); Mike Ruta's bracelets of recycled skateboards (page 136) to Karoline Fosse's simple wood and silver rings (page 17).

Wood jewelry? Just flip through the pages that follow to revel in the beauty and versatility of wood in the creative hands of jewelry artisans. The next time you utter the phrase "wood jewelry," I'll bet you won't end it with a questioning lilt in your voice.

Wood jewelry!

Wood Jewelry
BASICS

WOOD CHARACTERISTICS

Each species of wood has qualities that make it more or less desirable as a material for jewelry. You'll want to consider them carefully as you marvel at all the beautiful colors and grain patterns that are available. These qualities include hardness/density, toughness, color, grain, and figure.

Hardwoods and Softwoods

Scientifically speaking, *hardwoods* differ from *softwoods* in how they release their seeds. Hardwoods protect their seeds in nuts and pits instead of letting loose naked seeds, as pines do from their cones.

Hardwoods generally wear better as jewelry, and they often have more interesting grain patterns and colors. However, softwoods offer some distinct advantages even though they can't develop as much sheen as the harder species. If you intend to paint or decorate the wood, for example, basswood or pine might be excellent choices because they are easier to shape and weigh less than other woods, and they provide neutral backgrounds. As you will see, the terms "hardwood" and "softwood" don't necessarily provide reliable clues: basswood, a hardwood, is softer than most pine, a softwood.

Wood Grain

Talking about grain in wood can get a little confusing, so some basic definitions will help. *Grain* refers to the contrast between wood that grows early in the season (this wood has wider cells and is less dense) and wood that grows during the rest of the year, which is often lighter in color and harder. Those are the grain lines we can see. There are several different ways of talking about the direction of wood grain.

LONG GRAIN VS. CROSS GRAIN

In a long plank, the grain roughly parallels the long dimension of the plank. That's called *long grain*. The direction perpendicular to the long grain is called *cross grain*. A miter saw always works across the grain; it's a crosscut saw. A saw designed to cut with the grain is called a ripsaw.

LONG GRAIN VS. END GRAIN

In that same long plank, the four long surfaces are made up of *long grain*, while the two ends are (need I say it?) *end grain*.

LONG GRAIN VS. SHORT GRAIN

Short grain is long grain that's been cut short. If you drill a large hole near one end of the plank, *short grain* remains between the hole and the end of the plank.

WITH THE GRAIN VS. AGAINST THE GRAIN

One way we use these two terms is to indicate the same thing as long grain and cross grain. We sand with the grain, for example, not across or against the grain.

The more important use of these terms indicates the direction in which an edge tool (knife, chisel, or plane) should move along the wood surface. Working *with the grain* avoids tearing up the wood fibers and produces a smooth surface. The grain never runs perfectly parallel with the edges of a plank; it always "runs out" somewhere, in effect leaving the plank. The direction in which the grain seems to be moving as it runs out of a surface is called *with the grain* on that surface. Photo 1 shows the grain direction on each edge of the plank.

Photo 1

You can often feel which way the grain runs by brushing your fingers (or the back of them if they're calloused) back and forth along the grain. You'll notice that the wood surface is smooth in one direction (*with the grain*) and resists your skin in the other (*against the grain*). Now you can understand why a wooden disc has four different "with the grain" areas on its curved surface (photo 2).

Photo 2

Hardness and Density

In general, harder wood can be polished to a higher sheen than softer wood. Species like ebony and cocobola (page 11) shine nicely after they're sanded with fine sandpaper, and they may need no sanding at all if the pieces have been shaped carefully with sharp tools. Hardwood is, of course, more difficult to work with hand tools, but the results are usually worth the extra time and effort. Once polished, the pieces resist dents and damage while you're working with them or wearing them.

It might seem that hardness and density would always go together, and usually they do, but a hardwood with large pores, such as red oak, is less dense than a fine-grained hardwood. Higher density wood, once polished, has a smoother surface than less dense species.

Toughness

Toughness refers to a wood's resistance to splitting. If you have created an area of short grain in your piece, splitting should concern you. Wood splits with the grain, not across it—a phenomenon you experience when splitting wood for your fireplace—so the area of short grain is weaker than the long grain areas.

Some woods, such as bubinga and koa, have interlocking grain in which the fibers seem to wind around each other. The fibers of other woods have strong bonds along their grain. Experiment with the materials you're using to get a sense of their resistance to splitting, and use them accordingly. You may want to move a hole farther from an edge, for instance, and you would certainly avoid split-prone wood when making a bracelet.

Color, Grain, and Figure

Each species of wood has its characteristic color, and the colors can vary widely, from black to white and nearly every color except blue. Many woods display two distinct though related colors. The difference comes from the different growth patterns in early wood and late wood. Consider the colors shown on the following pages, and check out the websites of hardwood retailers to get a sense of the wonderful variety of wood colors.

In addition to the overall color and differing grain colors, some hardwoods show what's known as *figure*. Figure is the general term for conditions such as those we call *curly*, *birdseye*, and *quilted* that result when the wood fibers take unexpected turns. In curly wood, for instance, the grain is wavy instead of straight. The surface of the board shows bands of light and dark, and those bands change color as your viewing angle changes. This quality is called *chatoyance*—we use the same term when we refer to fire in gemstones.

What causes any figure remains unknown, except in the case of curl in the wood below a branch. This reaction wood results from the weight of the branch compressing the fibers in the tree trunk and is confined to a relatively small area. Reaction wood often has pronounced figure that offers visual interest for jewelry.

Suggested Wood Species for Jewelry

Here is an illustrated list of some beautiful species that you might consider when designing wood jewelry or jewelry with wooden elements. Many common North American woods have been omitted to leave space for unfamiliar species. Scientific names are included because some common names are used unconventionally by certain dealers, and dealers have been known to make up attractive names for lesser-known species.

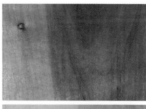

APPLE

finished/unfinished

Botanical Name: *Malus sylvestris*

Family: Rosaceae

Origin: Temperate regions of the world

Apple is a fruit tree that is fairly straight grained with a pinkish color. Domestic Apple tends to be knotty, while German Apple is normally clear (without knots). It works well with machine and hand tools, but it dulls knives and saws rather rapidly. When sanded, it is capable of taking an excellent finish.

BACOTE

unfinished

Origin: Central America

Bacote displays a medium brown color with nearly black streaks or graining. The tree is very small and yields only narrow planks. Its wood is very dense and has many properties similar to Rosewood.

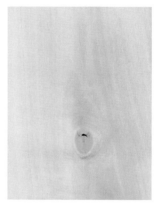

BASSWOOD

unfinished

Botanical Name: *Tilia americana*

Family: Tiliaceae

Origin: Eastern North America, with the Great Lakes states supplying 50% of the total yield

Straight grained with a light beige color, basswood is very easy to work with hand tools and is one of the most commonly used woods for carving and turning. It is very light weight.

BLACKWOOD (African)

finished

Botanical name: *Dalbergia melanoxylon*

Family: Leguminosae

One of the few true members of the Rosewood family from Africa, Blackwood comes in very small pieces 1 to 3 feet long and 1 to 6 inches wide. It is rarely available. Exceptionally heavy and dense, colored dark purple-brown with black streaks, Blackwood is difficult to work, so severely blunting of edges that it requires stellite or tungtsten carbide tipped saw teeth. Because of its density it finishes extremely well.

BLACKWOOD (Tasmanian or Australian)

finished

Botanical Name: *Acacia melanoxylon*

Family: Leguminosae

Origin: Australia, New Zealand, and Tasmania

A member of the Koa family that comes from New Zealand, Australia, and Tasmania. Like its relative, Hawaian Koa, this species can have a wide assortment of colors, and has similar working properties, but Tasmanian Blackwood tends to have fewer colors in an individual tree.

BUBINGA

finished

Botanical Name: *Guibourtia demeusei*

Family: Leuminosae

Origin: Cameroon, Gabon, and Zaire

It has been called African Rosewood, but bubinga is not a member of the rosewood family. The wood has a medium red-brown color, and the grain is very irregular or interlocked. It works well and is fairly easy to hand and machine tool, with difficulty being an occasional gum pocket. Bubinga is quite heavy.

BUTTERNUT

unfinished

Botanical Name: *Juglas cinera*

Family: Juglandaceae

Origin: USA and Canada

Butternut is the lightest colored member of the walnut family. It has a golden brown color, beautiful when finished. The density is lighter than walnut but it's a very nice wood for furniture. Butternut sands easily, but fuzzy fibers can be difficult to remove. Allow the first coat of finish to dry thoroughly, and sand again.

COCOBOLA

finished/unfinished

Botanical Name: *Dalbergia retusa*

Family: Leguminosae

Origin: West coast of Mexico and Central America

Like most rosewoods, Cocobola can have a wide array of colors, making it a beautiful wood. Most Cocobola comes in small pieces. A very heavy wood (heavier than water), it requires very sharp tools, but it can be sanded to a high sheen.

EBONY

finished

Botanical Name: *Diospyrus crassiflora* (African Ebony), *Diospyrus celebica* (Macassar Ebony)

Family: Ebenaceae

Origin: African: Nigeria, Ghana, and Zaire. Macassar: The Celebes Islands

Ebony is believed to be the darkest wood in the world, an extremely dense wood that will sink in water. The highest quality Ebony is pure black, but it can also have brown streaks. Macassar Ebony has heavy brown streaking.

ENGLISH SYCAMORE

finished/unfinished

Botanical Name: *Acer campestre*

Family: Aceraceae

Origin: Central Europe and the UK

English Sycamore is the whitest of the maples, and is also known as European Maple. It produces whiter and wider boards without heart than any North American maple. It sometimes exhibits heavy figure suitable for musical instruments. Of medium density, it finishes well and carves easily.

HOLLY

finished/unfinished

Botanical Name: *Ilex opaca*

Family: Aquifoliaceae

Origin: North America

Holly is a creamy-white wood that normally comes in smaller boards and tends to have a great many defects. Jewelers will experience no difficulties from defects. Quite dense with a fine even texture, it attains an excellent finish. Holly carves well, even though the wood is very hard.

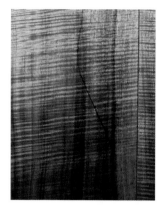

KOA

finished

Botanical Name: *Acacia koa*

Family: Leguminosae

Origin: Hawaii

A medium-density wood that displays a wide range of colors, koa grows only in Hawaii. The koa forests, essential to the ecology of the islands, have been reduced by over-harvesting, but reforestation projects are underway. Because of its scarcity and beauty, koa is expensive, and jewelers might consider using veneer instead of solid wood. One log yields more than thirty times as much surface area as veneer than as one-inch-thick planks.

OLIVE

finished

Botanical Name: *Olea hochstetteri*

Family: Oleaceae

Origin: East Africa, and Italy

Olive has irregular grey, brown, and black streaks, giving the wood a marbled appearance. Although its texture is fine and even, olive has interlocked grain that makes it difficult to carve. It is a dense wood that can be polished to a fine sheen.

PADUAK

finished

Botanical Name: *Pterocarpus soyauxii*

Family: Leguminosae

Origin: Central and west tropical Africa

The heartwood is vivid red or orange-red, but it gradually turns to dark purple-brown after it has been exposed to light and air. Paduak has a moderately coarse texture that finishes well. Its resin and dust are allergenic.

PEAR

finished/unfinished

Botanical name: *Pyrus communis*

Family: Rosaceae

Origin: Europe, UK, and western Asia

The heartwood has a pinkish-brown color, with straight, very fine texture. It is available only in relatively small sizes. Medium heavy, but very hard, it is difficult to machine and carve, but it takes a beautiful polish after sanding.

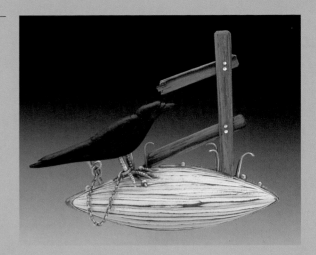

Marcia A. Macdonald
Mending Fences, 2002
7.6 x 8.9 x 1.9 cm
Sterling silver, wood, paint,
14-karat gold
PHOTO BY HAP SAKWA

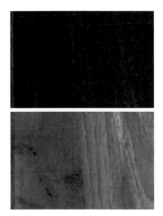

PERNAMBUCO (Brazilwood)

finished

Botanical name: *Caesalpinia echinata*

Family: Leguminosae

Origin: Brazil

The heartwood color is bright orange-red, which changes with exposure to red-brown. Pernambuco dulls edges rapidly, due in part to its extreme hardness and toughness. Those same qualities allow it to sand to a lustrous sheen. Close relatives of pernambuco vary in color all the way to black, as in pau ferro wood. Pernambuco is extremely endangered, and sources of supply will disappear soon, preferably because of governmental regulation.

Marcia A. Macdonald
You've got to use the right tools for the job, George, 2004
15.2 x 2.5 x 1.3 cm
Utensil handle, hair, silver, paint
PHOTO BY HAP SAKWA

PERUVIAN WALNUT

finished/unfinished

Botanical Name: *Juglans neotropica*

Family: Juglandaceae

Origin: South and Central America

In comparison with American (black) walnut, Peruvian walnut has a somewhat coarser texture and a decidedly darker, richer color. It works easily and sands to a silky luster.

Susan Chin
Peanut Body Earrings, 2005
8 x 2 x 1 cm
Ebony, 18-karat gold, 22-karat gold, Australian bolder opal; carved, pique worked, inlaid, fabricated, cast
PHOTO BY GEORGE POST

PINK IVORY (Red Ivorywood)

finished/unfinished

Botanical name: *Rhamnus zeyheri*

Family: Rhamnaceae

Origin: South and southeast Africa

As its name suggests, pink ivory is heavy, hard, and difficult to work with hand tools, dulling their edges rather quickly. The heartwood is yellow-brown with a red-gold luster.

RED NARRA

finished/unfinished

Botanical name: *Pterocarpus indicus*

Family: Leguminosae

Origin: Philippines

A trade name for a variety of Amboyna that grows in Cagayan, Philippines. Red Narra often displays good figure, retains its red color, and takes an excellent polish. It is a medium-weight wood that works easily with hand tools.

ZEBRANO, ZEBRAWOOD

finished/unfinished

Botanical Name: *Microberlinia brazzavillensis*

Family: Leguminosae

Origin: West Africa, chiefly Gabon and Cameroon Republic

Zebrano heartwood is a light golden-yellow with narrow veining or streaks of dark brown to almost black. The grain is so interlocked and has so much difference between hard and soft grain that it is nearly impossible to plane well by machine. Sanding seems to be the only way of working the wood successfully. It has a coarse texture, but can attain a lustrous surface.

PURPLEHEART

finished/unfinished

Botanical name: *Peltogyne pubescens*

Family: Leguminosae

Origin: Central America and tropical South America

One of the truly purple woods, it is brightest when freshly sawn or planed, gradually turning dark purple-brown. Lacquer finish may preserve the purple color. Purpleheart is easily scorched by circular saws and even sanding belts because of a gummy resin released by heat. Hard and heavy, it dulls tool edges, but it can be sanded to a high finish.

WENGE

finished/unfinished

Botanical Name: *Millettia laurentii*

Family: Leguminosae

Origin: mostly Zaire, also Cameroon Republic and Gabon

The heartwood is dark brown with closely-spaced, fine, almost black veins. Wenge is quite heavy and has a coarse texture. It works fairly well with hand tools and can be sanded to a fine finish.

Sources for Wood

If you think about it, you probably know a woodworker or wood turner. All woodworkers have more scrap than they know what to do with, so contacting someone who works with hardwoods is likely to produce plenty of potential jewelry material. Depending on what a particular woodworker makes, you may find scraps of exotic woods or domestic maple, cherry, and walnut. You can obtain the domestic species from local hardwood suppliers and even from some home improvement stores, but you will probably have to buy far more wood from these outlets than you'll need. Sure, one small plank won't drain your wallet, but how many earrings do you intend to make from an eight-foot board of walnut? Remember that it's always more efficient to buy wood in the thickness you'll be using.

The Internet has brought many lumber suppliers within easy reach, and some of them specialize in exotic species. Often the most beautiful woods are only available as small pieces, and their prices—like those of precious metals and gems—reflect their rarity. Find out if groups of woodworkers meet in your area. A wood turners' club might help you find pieces of beautiful hardwood. Bowl turners, especially, generate many small scraps. Members of the International Wood Collectors Society are excellent resources for information and, potentially, small samples of exotic hardwoods. The Society publishes a journal, *World of Wood* (that's right: *WoW*), which contains articles about wood species and listings of rare wood dealers. Sample copies are available in PDF format on its website.

Harvest Your Own Wood

Because only small pieces of wood are required for jewelry, you can harvest your own material. Before you fetch the pruning saw, keep in mind that whatever wood you gather should air-dry for at least six months, and you might have considerable waste from splitting and checking (splits across the grain). You'll need a band saw, and you'll have to be brave and careful while sawing. Buying dry wood is much easier, but if you still can't resist, here's how to proceed.

You'll find suitable "logs" almost anywhere. Fruit trees produce excellent wood for small applications, because it's generally fine grained and colorful. Since they're frequently trimmed, fruit trees yield plenty of stock if you're there at the right time. Choose the largest diameter branches you can find, because they contain more of the darker heartwood lying inside the light sapwood of the most recent growth. You needn't stick with the obvious fruitwoods, like apple, pear, and plum, either. Crabapple, for instance, has lovely yellow and red heartwood. Even common sumac produces beautiful heartwood in older bushes.

As soon as you gather your branches, cut them into manageable lengths—24 inches (61 cm) or shorter—then use a band saw to cut them lengthwise to thicknesses suitable for your purposes. The first cut you make, along the center of the limb, is the most hazardous; prop the limb so it won't twist during the cut. Then saw each half, flat side down, into small planks. Stack your planks to dry, with stickers (narrow wooden spacers) between the layers, until you're ready to use them.

You'll probably be ready to work with the planks as soon as they're sawn, but the wood will continue to shrink and change shape until it's thoroughly dry. Drier wood sands better and takes a higher polish. Drying times vary by species and thickness, but the rule of thumb is one year of air drying per inch (25 mm) of thickness. It's possible, but not highly recommended, to reduce that time considerably through judicious use of your kitchen oven set at a moderate temperature. Oven drying of green (freshly cut) wood can produce checks and other deformations if the drying proceeds too fast, so take it easy if you experiment. Denser woods are more prone to checking and developing interior stresses during drying.

**Dust mask and
safety goggles**

Dimensions of Wood, Plywood, and Veneer

Because it has grain, wood is measured in a particular way that differs from the art-world standard of height x width x depth. The length dimension of a piece of wood always follows the grain and is listed last. The thickness comes first and the width second. If you cut 1 inch (25 mm) from the end of a 2 x 4 (which actually measures 1½ inches x 3½ inches [38 mm x 89 mm]), the dimensions of the cut-off would be 1½ inches x 3½ inches x 1 inch (38 mm x 89 mm x 25 mm).

Plywood dimensions are commonly listed thickness first and then width x length, disregarding the face grain direction, but in applications where face grain direction is important, the convention follows that for solid wood. Veneer is sold by the square foot, with its thickness listed separately.

Woodworking Safety

Many crafts present risks to your health—and woodworking has its share—but you can lessen or prevent them. Even if you work with wood only occasionally, try to think about the following precautions as if you were a professional cabinetmaker.

Handling certain woods and breathing wood dust can cause allergic reactions. These will differ from person to person and from one wood to another, so pay attention to skin rashes and breathing problems while working with wood. Stop working if either of these reactions appears.

Always wear a dust mask or respirator when cutting and sanding wood. A disposable dust mask, which does a fair job of restricting dust from your lungs, is a reasonable choice if you seldom encounter wood dust. Still, its design can't fit everyone, and achieving a good seal between the mask and your face is nearly impossible. Respirators (there are many different kinds) have better sealing capabilities and a variety of filters to block both dust and some vapors.

It's a good idea to wear hearing protection when working with motorized tools or noise producers such as hammers. Prolonged exposure to these sounds will result in hearing loss, so wear earplugs, headphones, or both.

Power tools of all sorts can spit sharp projectiles directly into your eyes. Defeat them by wearing eye protection: goggles, safety glasses, or a full-face shield. Remember that other activities like hammering can produce flying chips, too.

Please remember the most important safety concept: Machines don't make mistakes. They always do what they can, given their current condition. Don't assume that the table saw blade is absolutely vertical, much less sharp, and don't assume that the drill press table is locked in place. Learn how to operate power tools, then watch, listen, and feel as you use them to find out how they work best. Finally, try to understand the forces involved in each tool, so that you can imagine, rather than experience, what might happen.

WOODWORKING TECHNIQUES

This small section can't teach every woodworking technique, of course, but it can present the special practices that a jeweler needs to know to create wooden jewelry or wooden parts for metal jewelry. And that's just what it does.

Creating Small Pieces

Jewelers and crafters are used to working with small objects. In woodworking, though, you often begin with a larger piece that must be reduced until it's close to the finished size. It's preferable to buy wood that's already milled to a thickness and width close to what you need. If that's not possible, you have several alternatives.

Remember that all woodworking can be done with hand tools alone; you don't need a fully equipped wood shop to fashion jewelry-size wooden pieces. In fact, it's often more efficient to cut out a blank with a handsaw instead of adjusting and setting a power saw. Hand tools are certainly safer, and mistakes happen much more slowly when you're using them—an important consideration.

If you have access to a miter saw, band saw, or table saw, you can use it to make blanks of the right size. Don't be shy about asking for help. Terror is a healthy response to a whirling metal object! If you're uncomfortable using a motorized saw, ask someone to cut your wood for you.

When using a miter saw, try to clamp your piece of wood to the saw's fence, and keep your hands away from the blade. A band saw is much safer than a

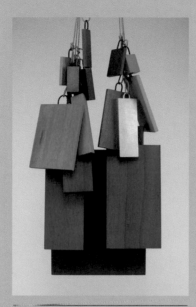

Julia Turner
Blue Box Pendant, 2006
12 x 9 x 3 cm
Maple, stain, steel, linen,
18-karat gold
PHOTO BY ARTIST

Judy Ditmer
Earrings, 2005
4 x 2.5 x .75 cm
Wenge wood, panga-panga, niobium,
resin, black onyx, brass; hand turned, cut,
shaped, reassembled
PHOTO BY ARTIST

Seth Papac
unlock, 2007
10 x 7.5 x 1.5 cm
Black and white ebony, fiber glass, sterling silver; hand fabricated,
riveted, oxidized
PHOTO BY MARIA PHILLIPS

Karoline Fosse
Untitled, 2004
Largest: 5.5 x 3 x 1 cm
Smallest: 4.3 x 2.2 x 1 cm
Wood, silver
PHOTO BY FEDERICO CAVICCHIOLI

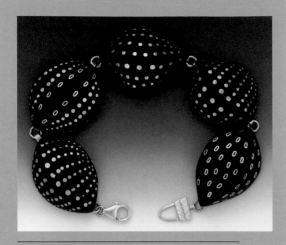

Susan Chin
Untitled Bracelet–Ebony Pods, 2006
14 x 3 x 2 cm
Ebony, 18-karat gold; carved, piqueworked,
inlaid, fabricated, riveted
PHOTO BY GEORGE POST

Paul McEwan
Egyptian, 2006
2.5 x 10.3 x 10.3 cm
Ebony, orange conkerberry;
hand fabricated
PHOTO BY ARTIST
COURTESY OF THE LINDA
TEAGUE COLLECTION

table saw when you're working with small pieces. You'll want to improvise a "zero tolerance" throat plate to reduce the size of the hole around the blade of a band saw. To do so, push a piece of plywood or a flat board, about 18 inches (45.7 cm) long, into the blade until its front edge is well beyond the blade—

Zero tolerance throat plate

about 5 inches (12.7 cm). Then clamp the plywood or board to the saw table. Now only sawdust can fall into the machinery.

Since the band saw blade runs vertically into the table, it won't throw pieces around the shop as a table saw can. Your main concern should be to make sure the wood you're sawing is support-ed directly below the saw cut, so the wood won't tilt suddenly and break the blade. The rule of thumb is to have wood touching the table on both sides of the band saw blade.

If you choose to crosscut small pieces on a table saw, use a miter gauge to help support the piece you're cutting. Avoid ripping small pieces on a table saw. (Rip sawing is cutting along the

wood grain rather than across it.) Use a band saw instead.

Mount a "splitter" behind the table saw blade, and keep scraps off the saw table to make sure that pieces of wood can't climb up on top of the blade. When that happens, the blade propels the wood at great speed directly toward you. If I've made you scared to use a table saw to cut small pieces, I've done my job.

Holding the Work

To hand saw, shape, or carve wood efficiently, you need a way to hold it in place. You shouldn't use one hand on the work and one hand on the tool for two reasons. First, it's usually much easier to control a tool such as a saw or a rasp with two hands. Second, sharp steel tools, if not kept on leashes, seem to enjoy attacking human soft tissue.

A wood vise works well, but a small metal vise mounted on a work table is probably better for small pieces because you can work on them from more angles. Use double-stick tape to attach thin pieces of pine or basswood to the jaw faces so the faces won't mar your work.

If you can extend part of the work piece past the edge of your bench, sometimes a clamp will do the trick. You can use jeweler's tools made to hold small objects, as long as you protect the wood from the metal jaws of pliers, for instance. C-clamps, spring clamps, bar clamps, and griplock pliers all have a place in the arsenal of controlling tools. As a final alternative, when nothing else will work, wear "cut resistant" Kevlar gloves.

Glue

Glue has many uses in woodworking. With it, you can adhere small pieces of wood together to create larger pieces, create laminations, and repair broken pieces.

You can use glue to hold pieces of wood together as long as their surfaces are flat and you're gluing long grain to long grain. End grain doesn't glue well because the glue soaks in and "starves" the joint. Woodworking glue doesn't bridge gaps well either, so the wood surfaces must meet closely. Use clamping pads (scrap pieces of wood) to protect your work from the clamps. Clamp across the joint to hold the pieces while the glue cures—about 30 minutes at room temperature.

In the case of a break, don't try to clean up the wood surfaces. Apply a small amount of yellow woodworking glue to the broken surface, and press the two pieces together exactly as they were before. Hold them tightly for five minutes or so, then lay the repaired piece in a safe place for an hour before you start working on it again.

To glue metal to wood, use a two-part epoxy that's formulated for those two materials. Follow the directions carefully; the strength of the joint depends on how well the resin and hardener are mixed.

Wood vise

Adapted metal vise

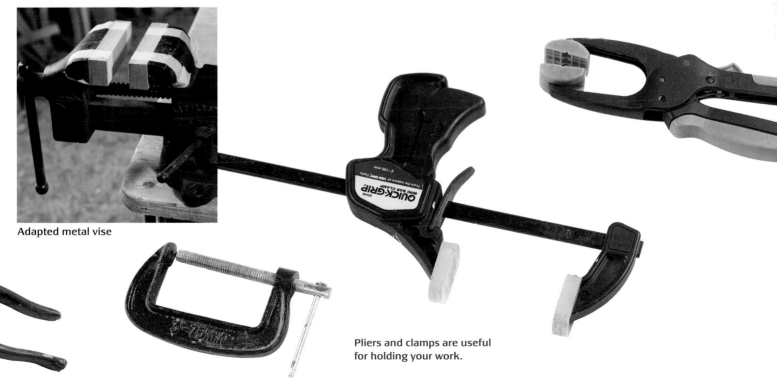

Pliers and clamps are useful
for holding your work.

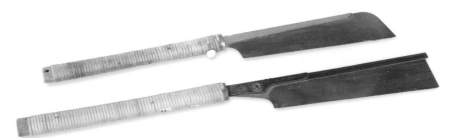

Dozuki saws

Rough Shaping

For most wooden jewelry work, you begin with a rectilinear piece of wood. The first steps toward a beautiful wooden object consist of a controlled hacking away at the rectilinear solid in order to reach the smooth and elegant path to glowing finished beauty. This section describes ways of hacking.

SAWING

To hand saw straight cuts in wood, use a small handsaw or a Japanese dozuki saw. Western handsaws work on the push stroke, so they require more force and remove more wood. Japanese saws cut on the pull stroke, so their blades can be thinner, with less tooth set, which results in less wood being removed. "Tooth set" refers to the amount the saw teeth are bent to create a space (the kerf) for the blade body to pass through. Support the work by securing it in a vise or by clamping it to the edge of a work table.

Coping saw and handsaw

For curved cuts, use a coping saw, which looks like a jeweler's saw but doesn't have its adjustability. As with a jeweler's saw, the teeth on a coping saw blade should point toward the handle so they cut on the pull stroke. Check the direction by running your finger along the teeth. They should catch when your finger moves away from the handle. Cutting on the pull stroke puts direct tension on the blade and makes the saw easier to control.

To cut out an inside shape, draw the shape of the opening on the wood, drill a hole large enough for the coping saw blade, just inside the line, and thread the blade through the hole, as you would with a jeweler's saw blade. Support the work with a jeweler's bench pin as you saw. If you have access to a drill press, consider boring out as much waste from an inside opening as you can before refining the shape with a coping saw or rasp.

A scroll saw (jig saw) makes curved cuts more quickly than a handsaw. Its motor moves a jeweler's blade, held at the ends of two arms, up and down through a stationary table. Imagine a jeweler's saw or coping saw that's powered unerringly by a motor instead of by your hand; a scroll saw leaves both your hands available to move the work piece. Don't make the common mistake of equating a saber saw with a scroll saw; a saber saw has no place in cutting small pieces for jewelry.

MAKING HOLES

You have several choices for cutting circular holes up to about 1 inch (25 mm) in diameter: brace and auger bits, twist drill bits, spade bits, multispur bits, and Forstner bits. While a traditional brace and auger bit is powered manually, it's still an efficient tool for boring a few holes. Remember to drill only until the bit's screw point emerges from the other side of the wood. Then finish the hole from that side. (Use the same method with some power-driven bits as well.) Because they've fallen out of favor, braces and auger bits probably won't be available at your local home improvement store. You'll have better luck looking in secondhand stores or at flea markets.

Very small twist drill bits can be powered by a chuck on a flexible shaft tool, by a small, motorized cutting tool, or by a handheld drill. Twist drill bits for metal are made as large as 1½ inches (38 mm) in diameter, but you'll rarely see one larger than ⅜ inch (10 mm) used for woodworking. There are better options for cutting large holes in wood, as you'll see. Twist drills excel at drilling small holes. Be aware that tiny chips from drilling can get caught in the flutes, so if your bit stops cutting easily, pull it part way out of the hole, let the chips fall out, and begin drilling again.

A spade bit consists of a shaft with a flat blade that includes two sharpened edges and a leading point between them. You can use a spade bit up to 1 inch (25 mm) wide with an electric drill, but make sure you clamp the workpiece over a layer of scrap wood.

If you have access to a drill press, use multispur and Forstner bits to speed up the process of making ¾-inch (19 mm) to 4-inch (102 mm) holes. Multispur and Forstner bits have small center spurs that hold the bit in place as it starts to bore. Multispur bits have sawlike teeth around their perimeters and two blades for removing wood from the middle of the hole. The small spurs at the outside ends of a Forstner bit's two blades score the wood before the blades start tearing away at the rest of the hole. Forstner bits make the cleanest holes, but they're also the most expensive of these alternatives.

Holes greater than 2 inches (51 mm) in diameter—for example, the holes you might cut if you were making wooden bracelets—are commonly cut with a hole saw mounted in a drill press. The saw teeth on the thin, circular rim of a hole saw cut the circumference of a hole. A twist drill in its center keeps the hole saw from skating around. The depth of cut is limited by the height of the outer rim of the hole saw, but most hole saws cut deeply enough for jewelry purposes. At the end of the cut, a round plug of wood remains inside the hole saw and must be pushed out before another hole can be cut. When using any kind of drill bit, provide a backing board under your workpiece to minimize tear-out on the bottom surface of the wood. It's best to clamp the workpiece to the backing board, but that's not always possible with small pieces.

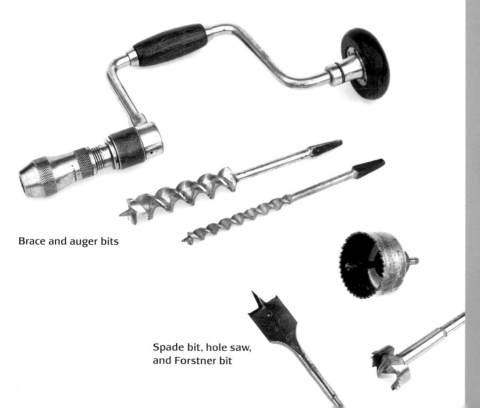

Brace and auger bits

Spade bit, hole saw, and Forstner bit

Sharon Church
Shimmer, 2004
16 x 5 x 3.8 cm
Boxwood, diamonds, sterling silver, buttermilk paint, lacquer; carved, oxidized
PHOTO BY JACK RAMSDALE
COLLECTION OF THE NATIONAL GALLERY OF AUSTRALIA, CANBERRA

James Roadman
Untitled, 2006
3 x 21 x .8 cm
Sterling silver, maple, mahogany, cherry, poplar, rosewood
PHOTO BY ARTIST

Bruce Metcalf
Costa Rican with Lips, 2004-06
30.5 x 12.5 cm
14-karat yellow gold, 18-karat yellow gold, 24-karat gold-plated brass, painted maple, 24-karat gold leaf; carved, painted, fabricated, chased, repoussé
PHOTO BY ARTIST
COURTESY OF CHARON KRANSEN ARTS, NEW YORK CITY, NEW YORK

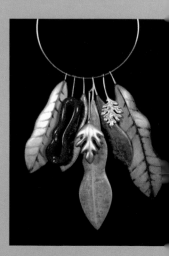

Refining and Smoothing Forms

After you've roughed out a form, you can refine it in three ways: abrade it with rasps and files, use a power sander, or carve it.

RASPS AND FILES

Rasps have individual teeth rather than the series of milled lines that are found on files. Use rasps before files because they remove wood more quickly and leave a rougher surface. Wood rasps are made in three basic shapes: flat, half-round, and round. A popular and inexpensive alternative is the four-in-hand rasp; it has one flat and one oval side, and each side has a file section and a rasp section.

The best type of rasp is the Nicholson pattern rasp. Its teeth are distributed in a random pattern over its flat/oval length and get smaller as they near the end of the rasp. These rasps cut aggressively and produce smoother surfaces than other rasps. They come in two grades, #49 and #50; the latter makes a smoother cut.

Files sold for woodworking are simply large metal files with bastard and mill patterns. There's no reason you can't use your rougher jeweler's files on your wood pieces, too, but if you're going to do much woodworking, invest in woodworking files. To keep the cutters unclogged, use a file comb regularly on both wood files and metal files.

POWER SANDERS

Hand pieces on powered flexible shafts and small, motorized cutting tools are familiar to most jewelers. The burrs, grinding discs, and sanding discs and drums made for these tools can make quick work of refining and detailing wood jewelry. If you're used to working with them on metal, apply lighter pressure on wood, or you'll remove more wood than you intend to. Remember to work with the grain when using these tools.

CARVING TOOLS

Carving tools—including knives, carving gouges, and chisels—offer a more satisfying and quieter way of refining your piece than the aforementioned methods. In addition, these cutting tools leave smooth, burnished surfaces that may not require any further sanding, depending on your skill and the texture you desire to create.

Carving tools must be very sharp to achieve smooth surfaces and to make safe cuts. It's easy to feel the difference—a sharp gouge or knife slides through the wood instead of hacking its way. If you intend to do a lot of carving, it's well worth the effort to learn how to sharpen your own carving tools.

KNIVES

You'll find a bewildering variety of carving knives available. Before buying a whole set, try a straight-bladed knife and a curved knife; these may turn out to be all you need. The usual advice about hand tools applies here: buy the best you can afford, even if that means buying fewer tools at first. The major difference between cheap tools and the best tools is the quality of their steel. Better tools are easier to sharpen and don't have to be sharpened as often. Good carving knives are also fixed firmly in their handles, unlike pocketknives, which are more dangerous to use because they're difficult to control.

Rasp, Nicholson rasp, file, and file comb

Motorized cutting tool, sanding drums, and carving burrs

Carving knifes

Working Tip

Don't carve after you've sanded. Sanding leaves abrasive particles in the wood, and they will dull your carving tools by making tiny nicks in their edges.

CARVING GOUGES

Fine carving gouges have relatively thin blades capable of accepting sharp edges; the blades are mounted in straight handles. Gouges are categorized by their amount of curvature and by their width. Good gouges have curvatures marked from 3 (almost flat) to 11 (U-shaped) and on up to higher numbers for specialty gouges. Start with a few modest widths, in shapes that appeal to you, making sure to include a number 3 or 4. Palm gouges, which are short and have bulbous handles, are very suitable for carving jewelry-sized pieces, as are the small, straight-handled gouges with short blades. Both handle shapes allow you to control them well without having to grab the blade down near the bevel.

Your gouges should be sharp enough to cut shavings from the wood with hand pressure alone. A mallet would be overkill on the small pieces of wood used in jewelry. Always carve with your work piece firmly supported in a vise.

On an irregularly shaped piece of wood, the grain direction changes constantly.

Don't be confused or try to reason with a block of wood. Just carve carefully and pay attention to the task at hand. If the wood starts tearing out, try working in the opposite direction or holding the gouge at a skewed angle. You'll soon find the way the wood wants to be cut in that area. On convex surfaces, straight chisels and knives often work more easily than gouges. One more point: carving across the grain sometimes works when nothing else does. So much for rules.

SANDPAPER

The last step before giving your wood jewelry its final finish is sanding. Sanding determines how smooth the wood will look and feel. The quality of any final finish depends on the quality of the sanding job. Take your time, and sand every surface that needs it. Always sand with the grain, not across the grain (page 9).

The grit size of any sandpaper is expressed by a number that gets larger as the grit size diminishes. The abrasive particles on 220-grit sandpaper are the largest that can pass through a mesh that has 220 openings per square inch.

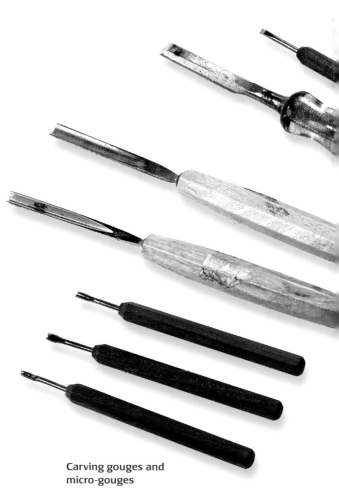

Carving gouges and micro-gouges

Catherine Truman
Yellow #3, 2006
8 x 11 x 4 cm
English lime wood, paint, Shu Niku ink;
hand-carved
PHOTO BY GRANT HANCOCK

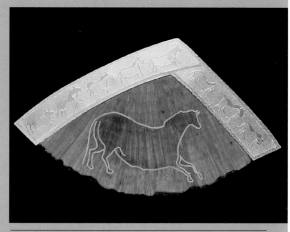

Ann L. Lumsden
Sympathetic Magic, 1991
8 x 13.5 x 1 cm
Sterling silver, fine silver, nickel silver,
briar wood, wood stain; roller
embossed, milled, inlaid, riveted
PHOTO BY JEREMY JONES

The larger the number of openings, the smaller they must be. Aluminum-oxide open-coat sanding sheets and discs intended for use on wood range from 36 grit to 400 grit. Wet-or-dry sandpaper is available in grits up to 2000. Grits below 60 and above 600 are excessively coarse and fine for sanding bare wood. Recently, abrasive manufacturers have adopted a more stringent standard to improve the quality of their sandpaper. A "P" in front of the number indicates that the new standard has been applied and that the size of the grit on the paper is within a narrow range.

Several kinds of grit, including flint and garnet, are used on sandpaper, but aluminum oxide stays sharper longer than others. Garnet does have one unique advantage: the crystals break into smaller particles as you use the paper, effectively ramping up to the next smaller (higher numbered) grit.

Start sanding with the lowest grit that seems reasonable. One limiting factor, depending on what you want to sand, is the thickness of the abrasive's backing—the paper itself. Lower grits usually have thicker backing that is difficult to bend and fit into small concave areas. For the sizes of the pieces required for the projects in this book, 120 or 150 grit is a good place to start. Whatever grit you begin with, use it to remove all the marks made by your tools, as well as all unwanted bumps and hollows. Change to a new sheet as soon as the grit starts to get dull; your time and energy are more valuable than a piece of paper.

White areas on wood indicate fuzzy fibers and indentations where the grit hasn't touched. Once all the white areas are gone and you see only clear wood grain, move up to the next finer grit. If you move up too soon, you're wasting time and effort.

If you start with 150-grit paper, 180 or 220 would come next, followed by 320, 400, and even 500 or 600 if you're that ambitious. The main job of a finer grit is to remove all the scratches from the previous grit.

Finishing

Many people like the feel of sanded wood without any finishing material on it. Others prefer surface finishes such as oil finish and polyurethane, which protect wood and generally deepen the color and contrast of the grain. The simplest finish you can apply is paste wax, which adds shine to the surface and protects it from occasional water damage. The beauty of the small pieces of wood used in jewelry depends on the subtle variation of their colors. Wood stain flattens those variations (that's one of its main jobs in the furniture industry), so one rarely sees wooden jewelry that has been stained.

An oil finish offers an easy surface treatment that doesn't hide the natural texture of the wood. Follow the manufacturer's directions, and apply two or three coats, waiting a day between coats. For each coat, wet the wood with oil, then wait for the oil to begin to "stiffen." When the oil slows your finger as you draw it over the surface, wipe up all of the extra oil with paper towels or cotton rags. Dry the wood thoroughly at each step to remove any dust and to keep the oil from *gunking up* (the technical term) at the edges. Rubbing with 0000 (pronounced "four ought") steel wool after the last coat hardens softens the

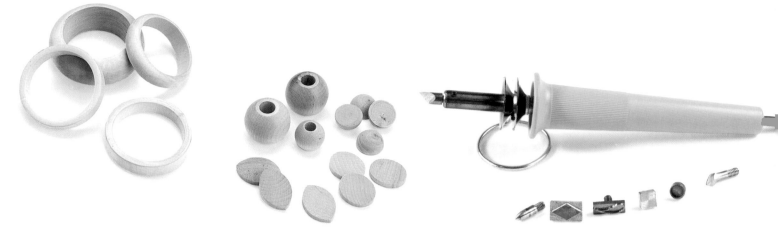

Commercial wood blanks for jewelry

Pyrography tool and pattern tips

glare and produces a very smooth surface. You can brighten the finish with paste wax if you wish.

Wipe-on polyurethane offers a somewhat harder finished surface than oil. Apply it in almost the same way as an oil finish except that you wipe it on and wipe it up at the same time. Sand between coats to smooth any hairy grain and to remove dust particles. You'll need to apply three coats to build a good finish, but you can probably apply all of them in one day.

Spraying clear lacquer or polyurethane from aerosol cans produces a good finish if you can mount the wooden part on a needle or a similar support. This allows you to spray the whole piece with each coat, avoiding oversprayed areas that will turn out rough. Make sure you practice on a well-sanded waste piece to learn how much finish you can apply without creating sags and drips. Sand with 220- or 320-grit sandpaper between coats. Follow the manufacturer's instructions carefully because they specify optimal tempera-

ture and humidity conditions as well as recoating times. Work outdoors if you can, and always wear a good respirator.

You can change the sheen of any finish by burnishing the surface after the finish coats harden. In this case, burnishing includes everything from rubbing the surface with 0000 steel wool, which produces a smooth, low sheen, to wet polishing with 2000-grit paper.

Woods such as basswood and poplar, which offer little visual interest themselves, are often used as substrates for painted surfaces. These softer hardwoods carve and sand easily, so they're perfect for sculptural treatments enhanced with paint. By the same token, it would be a shame to paint over curly maple, for example. Any painting technique or medium that can be adapted for tiny canvases will work for jewelry, and paint makes possible many surface treatments that are unavailable by other means.

PYROGRAPHY

The craft of decorative wood burning is a skill that is easy to begin and to

become proficient in, but also rewards continued study and experimentation. Pyrography offers a striking way of adding shading or pattern to your wood jewelry (pages 77 and 84.)

The basic tools of pyrography couldn't be much simpler: a shielded, electric heating element with a handle, and tips that fit on the heating element. The tips become hot enough to char the wood quickly, and when applied for a few seconds longer, produce black lines. Think of the color variations you've seen in a piece of toast, from very light brown to black. That entire color range is possible with pyrography, as are lines ranging from very thin to heavy.

You can easily dive in and start experimenting with a piece of scrap wood. Familiarity with your tool and the type of wood you're working with are your keys to success. Pyrography groups, formed to share their members' work and knowledge, offer a good source of help to beginners.

METALWORKING BASICS

Several projects in this book require metalworking skills as well as simple woodworking skills. The earrings shown on page 70 are perfect examples. These simple shapes are sawn from a silver sheet, then earring posts are soldered to them.

There's no reason to avoid projects that incorporate metalworking techniques. If you can cut wood, you can cut metal—as long as you use the proper tools. It's that simple. If you don't have an oxygen-acetylene torch for soldering, chances are you know someone who does or you have access to a jewelry repair person who will (for a small fee) do your soldering for you.

SAWING METAL

To saw metal, you need a jeweler's saw and saw blades, a bench pin, and sheet metal. What follows is a brief overview of the process; if you're new to it, practice on scrap sheet before you saw precious metals.

Place the metal on the bench pin. Position the saw blade vertically, perpendicular to the top surface of the metal. Move the saw frame up and down,

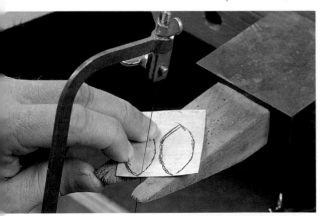

Sawing metal shapes

keeping the frame pointing straight forward. The teeth of the blade will cut the metal only on the downward stroke. Hold the saw in your hand lightly. Use it only as a guide; and do not exert pressure. The temptation to press too hard is great, and most beginning metalworkers break a lot of saw blades. Don't worry if this happens to you. Success and ease comes with practice. Stop frequently to relax your hand and arm muscles.

When making a curved cut, turn the metal, not the saw frame. To make a tight curved cut, simultaneously turn the metal and the saw while quickly moving the frame up and down to keep the blade from binding.

SOLDERING

Hot metalworking requires soldering. This process—applying heat, flux, and solder—permanently joins two pieces of metal. What follows is a brief overview of the soldering process. As with any working process, practice makes perfect.

The basic materials and tools you'll need are flux, solder (hard, medium, or easy grade), a heat-resistant work surface, a solder pick, and an oxygen-acetylene torch. You'll also need copper tongs to pick up the hot metal and a pot of warm pickle to remove the surface oxides that soldering creates.

Start by using a green scrubbing pad or abrasive paper to clean the two metal elements to be soldered. Then place the metal pieces on top of a heat-resistant surface such as firebrick. Position them so that the seam to be joined is flush, and apply flux to the seam.

Use the solder pick to pick up small pieces of solder (*pallions*), and position

them across the fluxed metal seam. Alternatively, you can use the torch to heat the small solder pieces on top of the firebrick until they ball up, and then use the pick to place them on the seam.

Light the torch, adjust it to a soft flame, and gently heat the area around the joint. The flux will bubble as the temperature of the metal rises. Use the pick to reposition any solder that moves off the seam or to add additional solder.

Soldering wire form

Continue heating the pieces until the solder flows bright and shiny around the joint. Turn off the torch. Use copper tongs to lift the soldered metal and quench it in a pickle bath. Remove the metal from the acid, rinse it in cold water, and dry it.

Different soldering operations may require the use of different soldering techniques. For example, when you're connecting a large joint that requires a lot of solder, using a length of wire solder rather than small solder pieces can be easier. The wire is placed on the joint after the metal is properly heated and is less likely to move out of position than pallions. Sweat soldering is beneficial when you need to attach a smaller metal piece on top of a larger one or when you're attaching jewelry findings.

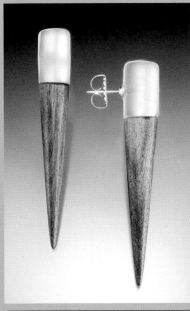

Karen Bachmann
Spikes, 2007
6.5 x 1 x 1 cm
Walnut, thermoplastic acrylic resin;
laminated, hand carved, sandblasted, polished
PHOTO BY RALPH GABRINER

John Ecuyer
Oceanic Armlet, 2007
9 x 6 cm
Ebonized sapele mahogany, brass, abalone shell; wood-turned, constructed
PHOTO BY JOHN ECUYER

Sharon Church
Oh, No!, 2006
15.3 x 8.2 x 5.1 cm
Boxwood, enamel, 14-karat yellow gold, diamonds, lacquer; carved
PHOTO BY KEN YANOVIAK

Carolyn A. Currin
Brooch and Earring Duo, 2005
30.5 x 14.6 x 7.6 cm
Brasswood, copper; pyrography
PHOTO BY LINDA DARTY

Tessa E. Rickard
Green Deer Fur Fetish, 2007
11 x 11 x 2 cm
Tiger ebony, sterling silver, dyed deer fur,
rubber; carved, glued, hand fabricated
PHOTO BY TIM CARPENTER

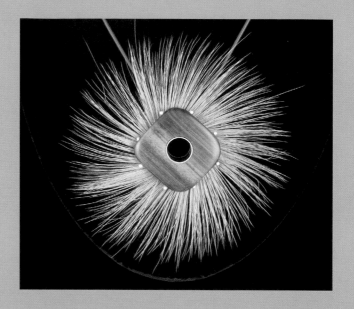

Kathryn Osgood
Golden Pod, 2004
10 x 4 x 3 cm
Wood, pearls, sterling silver,
23-karat gold leaf
PHOTO BY ROBERT DIAMANTE

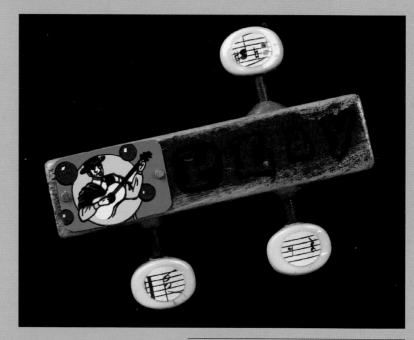

Opie O'Brien
Linda O'Brien
Play (Childs Play Series), 2006
7 x 8.9 x 1.3 cm
Wood blocks, guitar frets, rubber stamps,
rattle fragment, paper, pinback, wood
epoxy; stained, stamped, screwed
PHOTO BY STUDIO ROSS

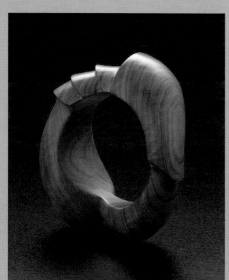

Norm Sartorius
Olive Bracelet, 2006
11 x 11 x 4.5 cm, variable
Olive wood, silver, oil finish;
hand sanded, refined, filed
PHOTO BY JIM OSBORN

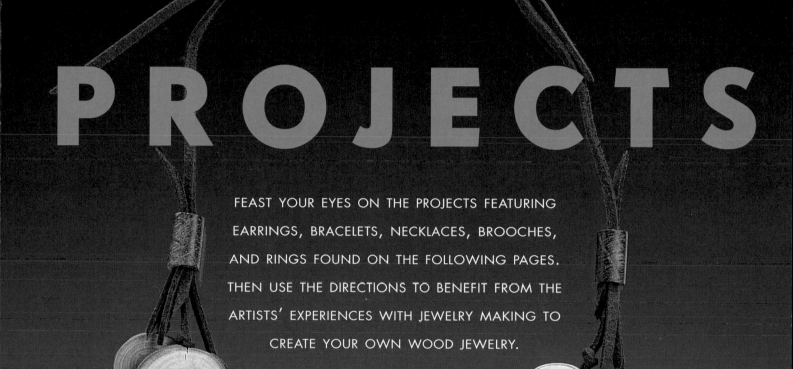

PROJECTS

FEAST YOUR EYES ON THE PROJECTS FEATURING
EARRINGS, BRACELETS, NECKLACES, BROOCHES,
AND RINGS FOUND ON THE FOLLOWING PAGES.
THEN USE THE DIRECTIONS TO BENEFIT FROM THE
ARTISTS' EXPERIENCES WITH JEWELRY MAKING TO
CREATE YOUR OWN WOOD JEWELRY.

Bird in a Tree Necklace

ARTIST
Georgie Ann Jaggers

GORGEOUS WOODEN BEADS HAVE BEEN MAKING THEIR WAY INTO THE MARKETPLACE FOR SEVERAL YEARS, AND YOUR CHOICES AREN'T LIMITED SOLELY TO SANDALWOOD. GO AHEAD—INDULGE YOUR PASSION FOR BEADS, AND AMASS A WIDE VARIETY OF THEM FOR THIS AND FUTURE NECKLACES.

MATERIALS

Flexible beading wire

2 crimp tubes

Assortment of small wooden beads*

20 to 30 seed beads, size 15

Glass bead

Sterling tree pendant

Pewter bird bead

Swarovski crystal

Apatite chips

Metal daisy spacers

Chain, about 12 inches (30.5 cm) long, with one link cut free

S-hook clasp

*The designer used palm wood, Manzanita twigs, Bayong saucers, coconut shell, sandalwood, rosewood, lotus seed wood, and boxwood in this necklace (photo A).

TOOLS

Steel ruler

Wire cutters

Needle-nose pliers

2 pairs of chain-nose pliers

PROCESS

1. Using the wire cutters, cut the flexible beading wire about 5 inches (12.7 cm) longer than the desired length of the necklace.

2. Place a crimp tube on one end, followed by a small wooden bead and 10 to 15 seed beads. Run the wire though the end link of the chain and back down though the crimp tube, leaving about 1 inch (25 mm) of excess wire beyond the tube. Use the needle-nose pliers to crush the crimp tube.

3. Begin stringing beads onto the wire, making sure that the first few beads cover the excess wire.

4. When all the beads have been strung, put on the other crimp tube, followed by 10 to 15 seed beads. Run the wire through the separated link of chain, through the crimp tube, and through a few more beads. Use the loose end of the wire to help pull all the slack out of the necklace. When everything is in place, use the needle-nose pliers to crush the crimp tube flat. Use the wire cutters to trim off the excess wire between beads.

5. Hook the S–hook clasp between the single link of chain and a link on the other side.

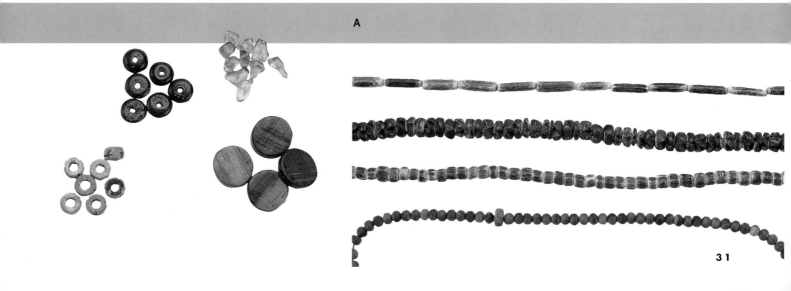

A

Oak & Amber Necklace

ARTIST
Vladimir Levestam

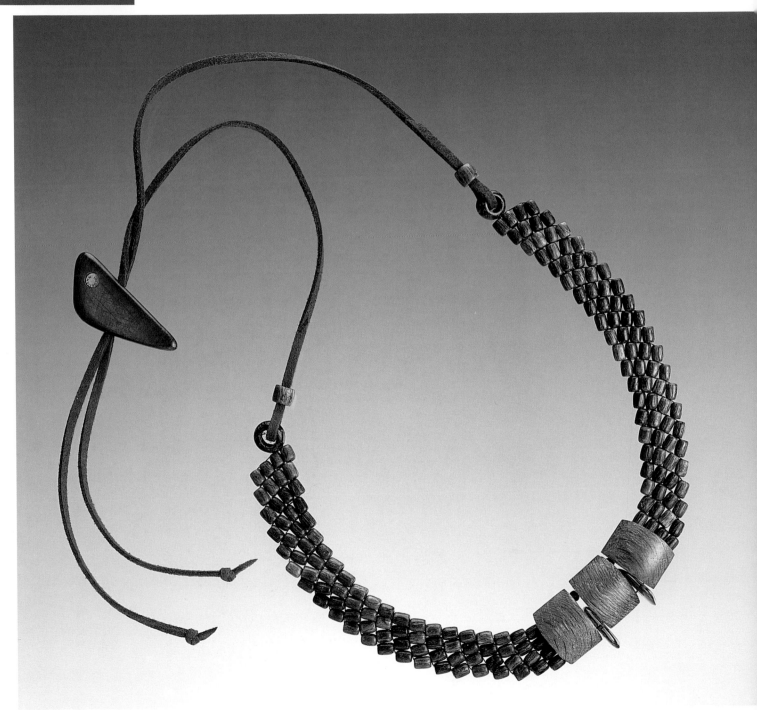

CONSTRUCTED ELEMENTS ARE COMBINED WITH COMMERCIAL WOOD BEADS TO CREATE A DRAPING NECKLACE. DON'T BE PUT OFF BY THE BEADWEAVING; IT'S A SIMPLE STITCH TO MASTER.

MATERIALS

Oak, ⅜ x ⅝ x 2 ¾ inches
(10 x 16 x 70 mm)

Oak, ¼ x ¾ x 1 ⅝ inches
(6 x 19 x 41 mm)

Sandpaper: 150, 220, 320, and
600 grit

Paste wax

Soft cloth

Heavy beading thread

2 flat amber beads, with 1- to
2-mm holes

168 cylindrical wooden beads,
4 mm diameter, 5 mm long, with
1-mm holes

2 wooden rings, 10 mm diameter,
5 mm thick, with 5-mm holes

2 wooden beads, 7 mm diameter,
6 mm thick, with 2-mm holes

Suede cord, 33 inches (83.8 cm) long*

*The designer used suede cord to
assemble this necklace. You can use
other cords, such as linen, hemp, or
leather, depending on the look you
wish to achieve.

TOOLS

Steel ruler, inch and millimeter

Table saw, miter saw, or handsaw

Vise

Pencil

Awl

Drill, with 1- and 2-mm drill bits

Drill bit, 5 mm (optional)

Beading needle

Scissors

Coping saw

PROCESS

Making the Middle Section

1. Cut the larger piece of oak into three equal pieces, using a handsaw, miter saw, or table saw.

2. Use sandpaper to make a curved surface on each piece of oak. The front should curve evenly from ⅛ inch (3 mm) thick at the ends to ⅝ inch (16 mm) in the middle. To produce the curved surface, begin by laying a sheet of 150-grit sandpaper on the work table. Hold it with one hand while you draw a piece of oak across it. Sand from close to the middle to an end, concentrating on removing more material near the end. Work toward both ends until you've made a smooth curve. Leave the edges flat and the corners sharp (photo A). Curve the other two pieces in the same way. After the curves are smooth, remove the scratch marks with 220- and 320-grit paper, again laid flat on the table (photo A).

A

3. Hold one of the oak pieces in the vise (with padded jaws), with one edge on top. Draw two lines across the edge, equidistant from the ends and ½ inch (13 mm) apart. Use the awl to make starting dimples, and drill two 1-mm holes through to the other edge (photo B). Drill holes in the other pieces in the same way.

4. Sand the oak pieces with 600-grit sandpaper, and finish them with a coat of paste wax buffed with a soft cloth.

5. Arrange the oak pieces in a row with their edges together. Using the beading needle, pull a length of beading thread through the upper holes. Pass the thread back through the lower holes, but include an amber bead between each pair of oak pieces. Tie a knot near the upper hole, thread the beading thread through the upper holes again, and pull it to hide the knot inside the first piece. Trim the thread close to the holes.

Brick Stitch

A brick stitch begins with a "ladder," in this case, four beads wide. Begin by passing the needle up through the first bead and down through the second. Then go up through the first bead again, completing a loop. One loop is sufficient (and that's what's shown in the diagram below, for easier reading), but using two loops results in a sturdier ladder.

After looping the first two beads together, go back through the second bead and up through the third bead. Loop the second and third beads together, and add the fourth bead in the same way, ending with the yarn going downward through the fourth bead.

To start the second row, go down through the fifth bead and up through the sixth. Loop the yarn over the threads connecting the third and fourth beads, then back down through the sixth bead again. The illustration shows the beads widely separated, but they should be pulled together, as shown in the project photo.

Stitch the rest of the beads in the same way, always moving the rows to the same side and shaping the curve as you go. Tie the thread ends to the first and last beads.

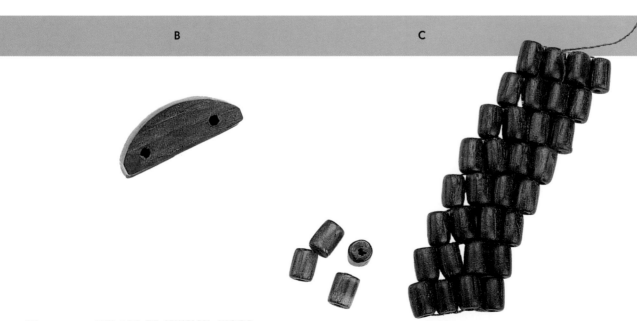

B

C

Making the Brick-Stitched Sides

6. To make the two curved pieces of the necklace, brick-stitch 21 rows with the 4-mm beads, each four small beads wide, with more tension on the thread when it connects the inside beads (photo C).

7. Using the needle and beading thread, tie the central piece of the necklace to the two side pieces. Do this by passing a length of thread through the upper holes of the central piece, then through the first bead of the bottom row of a sidepiece. Weave the thread back and forth through the second, third, and fourth beads. The thread will emerge from the fourth bead ready to go through the bottom holes of the central piece. Connect the other side piece, and tie the ends of the thread. Pull the knot inside one of the small beads, and trim the thread.

8. Add a wooden ring to the top of each side piece, using the needle and beading thread. Bind each ring to the two

inside beads of the ladder, going down through one bead, up through the other, and around the ring. Follow that path three times, then tie the yarn and hide the knot as before.

9. Cut two 19¾-inch (50 cm) pieces of suede cord. Pull 2½ inches (64 mm) of a suede cord through one of the 7-mm beads. Pass the cord through a ring and back through the bead. Pull the cord so the bead rests against the ring. Add the other suede cord in the same way.

Making the Toggle Clasp

10. On the thinner piece of oak, draw a triangle with sides 1⅝, 1, and ½ inches (41, 25, and 13 mm) long. Cut out the triangle with the coping saw or handsaw. Sand all surfaces of the triangular piece, beginning with 150 grit and ending with 220 grit. Round the edges and corners with the 220-grit paper (photo D).

11. With the pencil, mark the centers of the two longest edges. Draw a light pencil line across the face of the triangle

to help you sight from one mark to the other. Hold the triangle in the vise, and drill from one mark through to the mark on the other edge, using the 2-mm bit.

12. Sand the toggle with 320-grit and 600-grit sandpaper, and finish it with paste wax.

13. Feed the two loose ends of the suede cord through the hole in the toggle, and pull them through together. Adjust the length of the necklace, and tie knots in the cords about 4 inches (102 mm) beyond the toggle. Trim the cords, leaving 1¼-inch (32 mm) tips.

D

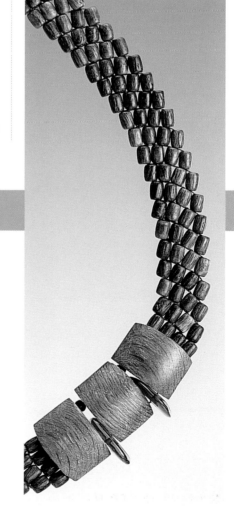

Ebony Scroll Ring

ARTIST
Bronwynn Lusted

BOLD—THERE'S NO OTHER WORD TO DESCRIBE THIS ATTENTION-GETTER OF A RING. ITS SIZE BELIES ITS LIGHTNESS ON YOUR HAND. IT'S PERFECT FOR AN EVENING COCKTAIL PARTY; JUST BE SURE TO GRASP THE STEM OF YOUR GLASS WITH YOUR RING HAND.

MATERIALS

Ebony wood, at least 1⅜ inches (35 mm) square x 1¾ inches (44 mm)*

Sandpaper: 60, 100, 220, 320, 800, and 1200 grit

Oil finish (optional)

Cotton rags (optional)

Steel wool, 0000 grade (optional)

Carnauba wax flakes (optional)

Paper towels (optional)

Choose a piece of ebony that is as free of cracks as possible.

TOOLS

Band saw, coping saw, or jeweler's saw

Steel ruler, inch and millimeter

Spade or Forstner bit, diameter to fit your ring size

Awl

Drill press or electric hand drill

Bar clamp

White pencil

Vise

Coping saw

Small, handheld rotary tool

Sanding drum, ½ inch (13 mm) diameter, with 60- and 100-grit sanding bands

Ball-shape burr, 1 mm

Small ceramic cup or bowl (optional)

Firm bristle brush for the rotary tool, 22 mm diameter (optional)

PROCESS

1. Trim the ebony to a block 1⅜ inches (35 mm) square x 1¾ inches (44 mm), using the band saw, hand saw, coping saw, or jeweler's saw.

2. Measure the inside diameter of one of your rings. To bore the finger hole, you'll need to find the spade or Forstner bit that is slightly smaller than your ring diameter. You will enlarge the hole to your finger size later. Sharpen the bit if necessary—even new spade bits often require sharpening.

3. Using the awl, mark the center of the finger hole on one of the 1⅜ inches x 1¾ inches (35 mm x 44 mm) faces of the ebony block, in other words, mark a long-grain face, not the end grain. Make sure to leave at least ¼ inch (6 mm) between the hole and the end of the block. Using the spade or Forstner bit and the drill press with a piece of scrap wood on its table, or a handheld drill, bore the finger hole. Use a bar clamp laid on the scrap wood to hold the block, helping to keep it in place and to keep it from spinning with the bit. Ebony is very hard, so the drilling will go slowly.

4. Using the white pencil, draw the shape of the ring onto the ebony. Make sure you allow 5 mm of wood for the ring band.

5. With the ring held in a vise, use the coping saw to trim the areas outside the line. Make sure that the cut stays perpendicular to the face of the block, and stay outside the line.

6. Draw the side-view outline on the ring blank, and saw outside the line as before (photo A on the next page).

7. Using the small, handheld rotary tool and the sanding drum with a 60-grit band, sand off the remaining excess wood to shape and smooth the ring's form (photo B on the next page). Refer often to the photograph comparing your progress to the intended form. Use the sanding drum to enlarge the hole to fit your finger firmly. Work carefully to avoid making the hole too large, and keep in mind that more sanding will be needed to make the inside surface smooth. The band of the finished ring should be ½ inch (13 mm) wide and ⅛ inch (3 mm) thick. When the hole is smooth and fits your finger very tightly, switch to the 100-grit band, and remove all the scratches made by the 60-grit band.

Working Tips

To avoid burning the wood from the heat built up by the friction of the bit, raise the bit out of the wood every few seconds. If the bit heats too much, its cutting edges will dull quickly.

Spade bits can stall when they near the bottom face of the wood. If this happens, turn the drill press off immediately, and raise the bit free of the wood. You can leave the hole as is, because the sides of the block will be trimmed off, leaving an open hole.

A   B

8. Using a small piece of 60-grit sandpaper, smooth the ring's form, and make sure that it's symmetrical from all viewing angles.

9. Use the white pencil to mark the scroll line on the ring's top, and clamp the ring in a well-padded vise. To cut the scroll groove, first secure the 1 mm round burr in the rotary tool. On a scrap of dense wood, practice using the burr by cutting a line to find the technique that works best for you. Hold the tool as close to the burr as possible, and brace your hand against the vise for more control. Try holding the tool in your fist, with the heel of your braced hand closer to the burr, and moving the burr in short strokes with your fingers only.

10. Continue to carve until the groove is a scant $^1/_{16}$ inch (1.6 mm) deep. Try to keep the bottom of the groove smooth and free of lumps.

11. Hand sand the inside of the groove with 100-grit sandpaper to refine the shape and smooth the square edges. Then sand the ring with 220-, 320-, 800-, and 1200-grit sandpapers. The ring should fit nicely when you've finished sanding with the 220-grit paper; after that, very little wood will be removed. Check for scratches after each grade of sandpaper.

12. You can use the oil finishing method described on page 24, but the designer recommends soaking the ring in carnauba wax.

Carnauba Wax Finish

Put carnauba wax flakes in a clean tin can or heatproof container. Place the container in a hot water bath to melt the wax. When the wax has completely melted, remove the container, and place the wood object in the melted wax. Return the container to the hot water for an additional 15 minutes. This allows the wood to warm and absorb the wax. Remove the container and use a spoon or tongs to remove the wood object. Wipe off excess wax with paper towels. Buff the waxed surface by hand or with a rotary tool and soft bristle brush attachment.

Golf Tee Bracelet

ARTIST
Karen J. Lauseng

FORE! YOUR CADDY (AND EVERYONE ELSE) WILL BE IMPRESSED WITH YOUR INVENTIVE USE FOR THESE HUMBLE MATERIALS. IF COLOR IS MORE TO YOUR LIKING, PAIR BRIGHTLY COLORED TEES WITH BRIGHT CABOCHONS.

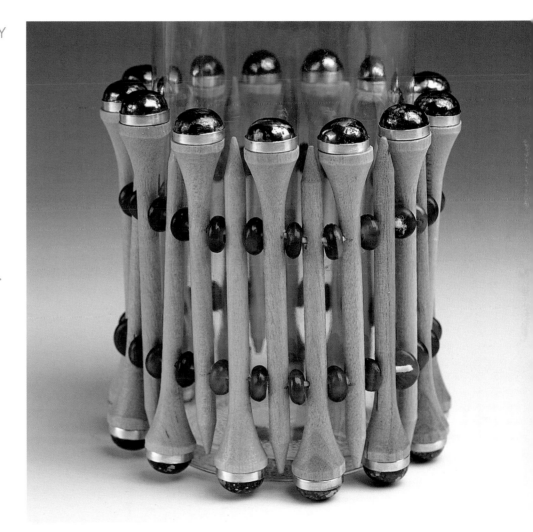

MATERIALS

26 wooden golf tees, 2 ¾ inches (70 mm) long*

Masking tape, ¾ inch (19 mm) wide

26 sterling silver bezel cups, 10 mm

26 escutcheon pins, 1.2 x 12.7 mm

Epoxy, two-part five-minute

26 pyrite cabochons, 10 mm

Elastic beading cord

52 horn rondelles, 6 mm

White glue

Using 26 golf tees will create a bracelet to fit an average woman's wrist. For a small wrist, use 24 tees. Twenty-eight golf tees will work well for a larger wrist.

TOOLS

Steel ruler

Small C-clamp

Awl

Drill with ¹⁄₁₆-inch (1.6 mm) drill bit

Small center punch

Hammer

Vise with padded jaws

Fine point permanent marker

Steel block or anvil

Burnisher

Scissors

PROCESS

1. Each golf tee must have two holes in it for the elastic cord, each ¾ inch (19 mm) from an end, and the holes must be parallel to each other. To measure the hole placement accurately, align an edge of a short piece of ¾-inch-wide (19 mm) masking tape with each end of a golf tee. Grip the head of the tee with a small C-clamp, and position the tee and C-clamp on the work table so the tee won't roll.

2. To guide the drill bit, use the awl to make indentations at the inner edges of the tape. Make sure that the indentations are exactly on the top centerline of the tee.

3. Use the drill and ¹⁄₁₆-inch (1.6 mm) drill bit to bore the two holes. Repeat to drill holes in the rest of the golf tees (photo A).

4. Hold the small center punch at the center of a sterling silver bezel cup, and tap once lightly with the hammer to create a small dimple. Hold the bezel cup on a piece of scrap wood, and drill a ¹⁄₁₆-inch (1.6 mm) hole through the bezel cup. Drill holes in the rest of the bezel cups (photo B).

5. Grip a golf tee, head up, in the vise with padded jaws. With the awl, press an indentation into the top center of the tee.

6. Use the fine point permanent marker to draw a mark ½ inch (13 mm) from the point of the ¹⁄₁₆-inch (1.6 mm) drill bit. Then drill a hole in the top center of the golf tee to the depth marked on the bit. Drill holes in the tops of the rest of the tees.

7. Flatten the point of an escutcheon pin by placing the pin on the steel block or anvil and hammering the point a couple of times with firm pressure. Repeat to flatten the rest of the pins.

8. Prepare a small quantity of the epoxy according to the manufacturer's instructions. Working quickly, put a little epoxy on the bottom of a bezel cup, and dip the point of an escutcheon pin into the epoxy, as well. Hold the bezel cup on top of a golf tee, and press the escutcheon pin firmly into the tee. Mount the rest of the bezel cups in the same way.

9. When the glue has cured, set the pyrite cabochons one at a time. Place one into a bezel. Hold the burnisher between your thumb and forefinger, and press the silver inward, working your way around the bezel. It may take several trips around the bezel to get a nice snug fit. For added strength, you may want to put a drop of epoxy inside the bezel cup before adding the stone (photo C).

10. Cut two pieces of elastic beading cord, each about 20 inches (51 cm) long. Knot one end of each cord, and begin stringing the tees. String both cords through a golf tee, and add a horn rondelle to each cord. Flip the next tee end for end, and add it to the cords, followed by another rondelle on each cord. String the rest of the golf tees and horn rondelles (photo D).

11. Tie the ends of the cords with square knots. Put a drop of white glue on each knot, and thread each end of the cords back through the adjacent tee. Trim the cords with scissors.

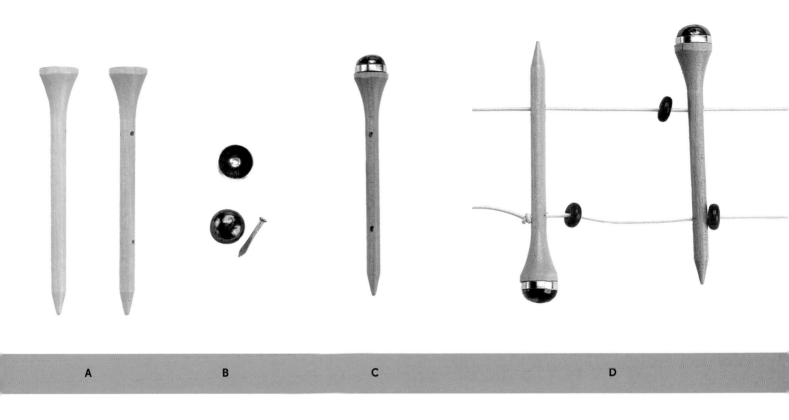

A   B   C   D

VARIATION:
Top your tees with
different materials to
suit your taste.

Granulation Earrings

ARTIST
Molly Dingledine

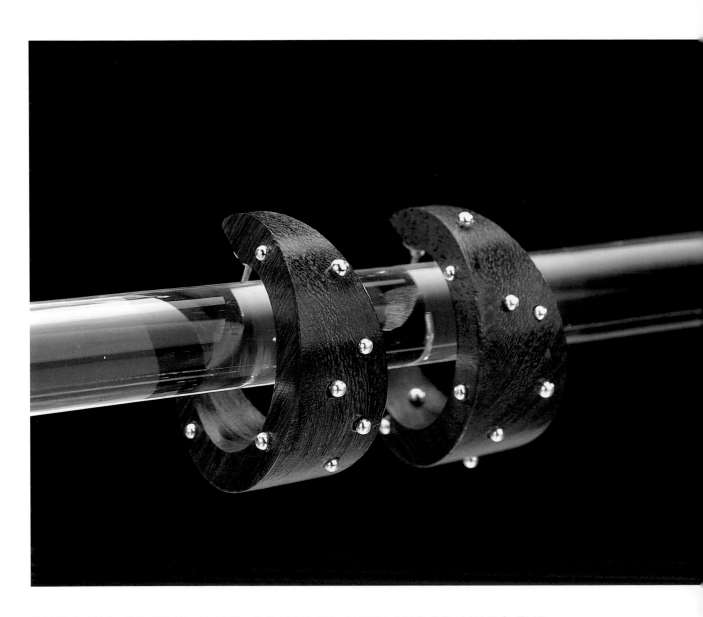

TINY BALLS OF FINE SILVER COMBINED WITH WOOD MIMIC THE

LOOK OF SILVER GRANULATION IN THIS PAIR OF EARRINGS.

MATERIALS

Premade wooden semi-disc
  earring forms*

Fine silver wire, 20 gauge

½-inch (13 mm) earring posts
  and backs

Flux

Solder

Pickling solution

Epoxy, two-part five-minute

*You can buy manufactured wooden
  earring forms from many jewelry
  supply sources (photo A).*

TOOLS

Steel ruler, inch and millimeter

Wire cutters

Tweezers

Oxygen-acetylene mini-torch

Soldering equipment

Hard plastic or glass bowl with water

Tiny ball burr to match the silver balls
  (see step 2)

Flexible shaft tool and #61 drill bit

PROCESS

1. In your head or on paper, decide what design you would like to create with the silver balls.

2. Cut several pieces of the 20-gauge fine silver wire, each about ¼ inch (6 mm) long. One at a time, pick up a piece of wire with the pair of tweezers, and use the oxygen-acetylene mini torch to ball up one end, leaving about ⅛ inch (3 mm) of straight wire. Drop the balled-up pieces into the bowl of water to cool (photo B).

3. Wherever you want a silver ball on your earrings, use the ball burr in the flexible shaft tool to carve out a round depression in the wood, no more than one-half sphere deep. Using the #61 drill bit in the flexible shaft tool, drill a shallow hole at the center of each depression.

4. Mix up a very small amount of the two-part epoxy. When the epoxy is thoroughly mixed, pick up a ball with your tweezers, dip the tip of the wire end into the epoxy, and push the wire into a hole. You've used enough epoxy if the ball doesn't fall out; if it does, pick up a little more and try again. There should be no epoxy around the edge of the depression.

5. Continue setting the silver balls into the wood until they are all in place. The epoxy will probably begin to cure before you're finished. Mix up a new batch in a different place with a new mixing stick.

6. After the epoxy has completely cured, drill short holes for the posts. Mix up another batch of epoxy, and set the ends of the earring posts into the wood.

A

B

Encircling Discs Necklace

ARTIST

Marcy Grant

ROUND AND
ROUND, THE
COLORS OF
EXOTIC WOODS
ENCIRCLE THE
NECK IN A
SLEEKLY MODERN
FASHION — NO
MUSS, NO
FUSSINESS.

MATERIALS

Variety of flat, rounded, wooden
 disc forms

Thick, stainless steel beading wire

Large crimp beads

Oval wooden toggle

TOOLS

Steel ruler, inch and millimeter

Drill press or handheld drill, with
 1- to 2-mm drill bit

Needle bead reamer

Wire cutters

2 beading clips

Crimping pliers

PROCESS

1. Find a variety of flat, rounded wooden
disc forms. To create interest, be sure to
select different types of woods of different shades and shapes.

2. To make a hole in the center of each
disc, use a drill press (or drill) and the
1- to 2-mm drill bit (photo A).

3. Use a needle bead reamer to file and
smooth the edges of the holes.

4. Arrange the discs in a circle for the
necklace, choosing dark and light
shades of wood in the composition.

5. With the wire cutters, cut two 30-inch
(76. 2 cm) lengths of thick, stainless
steel beading wire.

6. String the first strand of beading
wire through the arranged wood discs,
then clip the wire at one end with a
beading clip.

A

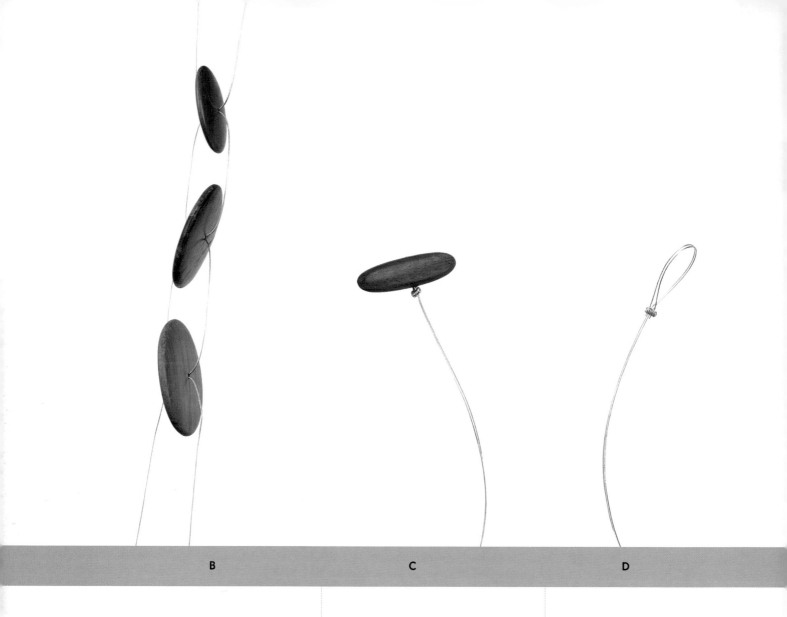

B

C

D

7. Start the second strand of beading wire by inserting the wire through the opposite side of the first strung disc. Proceed by stringing the wire into the opposite side of the second disc, creating a double-loop shape with the wire. Separate each pair of discs as you move along, spacing them ¼ inch (6 mm) apart (photo B).

8. After stringing the final disc, stop further movement by cinching the loose end of the necklace with the other beading clip.

9. With the drill press or handheld drill and bit, drill a 1- to 2-mm hole through the middle of the oval wooden toggle. At one end of the necklace, string both wires through a large crimp bead. Run the beading wires through the toggle and back through the crimp bead. Crush the bead with the crimping pliers, and trim the excess wire with wire cutters (photo C).

10. The other end of the necklace needs a loop to accommodate the wooden toggle. String a large crimp bead on the other end of the necklace. Create a loop

just large enough for the toggle to fit through, and loop back through the crimp bead. Crimp the bead with crimping pliers, and trim the excess wire with wire cutters (photo D). The length of the necklace will be between 17 and 20 inches (43.2 and 50.8 cm), depending on the sizes of the wooden discs, their spacing, and the flexibility of the wire.

Ebony Disc & Mixed Wood Pendant

ARTIST
Bronwynn Lusted

THIS PENDANT SHOWCASES A MIXED ARRAY OF WOOD SAMPLES. EXOTIC WOODS OR WOODS FROM YOUR LOCAL FOREST CAN BE USED TO CREATE THIS DYNAMIC PIECE.

MATERIALS

Ebony, ¼ x 2 ⅝ inches square (6 mm x 65 mm)

7 pieces of various woods, at least ¼ x ⅝ x 3 ½ to 5 inches (6 x 16 x 89 to 127 mm)*

Heavy paper, such as a manila file folder

Sandpaper: 60, 100, 150, 240, 360, 800, and 1200 grit

Oil finish (optional)

Cotton rags (optional)

Steel wool, 0000 grade (optional)

Carnauba wax, 4 to 8 ounces (113.4 to 226.8 grams) (optional)

Paper towels or tissues (optional)

Satin cord, ⅛ inch (3 mm) in diameter and 39 inches (100 cm) long

Black sewing thread

Black craft wire, 20 gauge, or 0.8 mm silver wire

Look for wood pen blanks to create this project. They're an ideal size and don't require much cutting to shape. African Ebony and Australian woods (brown mallee burl, grass tree, huon pine, sace she-oak, myrtle burl, black mulga, and red mallee root) are used in this pendant (photo A).

TOOLS

Steel ruler

White and black pencils

Scissors

Compass (optional)

Band saw or handsaw/coping saw/ jeweler's saw

Awl

Drill, with ¹⁄₁₆-inch (1.6 mm) and ¼-inch (6.4 mm) drill bits

Random orbital sander

Sanding block

Small ceramic bowl (optional)

Small, handheld rotary tool (optional)

Firm bristle brush, ⅞-inch (22.2 mm) diameter, for rotary tool (optional)

Sewing needle

Wire cutters

Flat-nose pliers

Round-nose pliers

PROCESS

1. On the piece of heavy paper, draw a template for your longest triangular piece, and cut it out. Trace the template on the various pieces of wood, using the white or black pencil. Use the white pencil and the compass to draw a 2 ⅝-inch (67 mm) diameter circle on the ebony. If you don't have a compass, find a suitable tumbler or can to trace.

2. Cut out the shapes, using the band saw, hand saw, coping saw, or jeweler's saw.

3. Find the center of the disc, use an awl to mark it deeply, and drill a ¼-inch (6 mm) hole through the disc (photo B). Remember to put a piece of scrap wood under the disc before drilling.

4. Along the edge of each triangular piece, mark a spot ⅜ to ½ inch (9.5 to

A   B

13 mm) from the narrow end. Use the awl to deepen the mark. Drill a ⅟₁₆-inch (1.6 mm) hole through each piece (photo C).

5. Using 60-grit sandpaper on the random orbital sander or the sanding block, sand the sawn pieces until you have a nice, round, ebony circle and the triangular shapes you like. Round or taper the ebony circle's edge, but leave at least ³⁄₃₂ inch (2.4 mm) flat. Gently curve the wide bottom ends of the triangles.

6. Hand sand the flat surfaces by rubbing them on 60-grit sandpaper placed on a flat work table. Make sure to keep the edges perpendicular to the front and back surfaces.

7. Use 100-grit sandpaper to remove all of the 60-grit scratches, then move on to 150 grit and 240 grit. Use 360-grit through 1200-grit paper to achieve a very smooth surface. Hold these papers in your hand so that they soften the edges and faces as you proceed. Remove all scratches from previous grits with the sandpaper you're using before moving on to the next grit.

8. You can use the oil finishing method described on page 24 or soak the pieces in carnauba wax (page 38).

9. Push the ends of the satin cord from back to front through the hole in the ebony disc. Tie the ends with a square knot, try on the pendant, and adjust the length of the cord. When the length feels comfortable, tighten the knot, and trim the cord ends ¾ inch (19 mm) from the knot. Wrap the ends around their adjacent cords, and sew them using the needle and black thread. Tie off and trim the thread. Pull the knot tight against the ebony disc, hiding the cord ends in the back.

10. Use the wire cutters to cut a 7-inch (17 cm) length of 20-gauge black craft wire or 0.8 mm silver wire. Arrange the triangular pieces, and thread the wire through them.

11. Hold the triangles flat on the table while you bend the wire ends back together to form a miniature wire coat hanger. Keep holding the triangles in place, and use the flat-nose pliers to pinch the wires and twist them together. The twisted portion should begin about ⅜ inch (10 mm) above the middle triangle and extend ⅞ inch (22 mm) in length. Using the round-nose pliers, bend the twisted section into a ¼-inch (6 mm) loop. Check to make sure that the doubled satin cord goes through the loop (photo D). Secure the end by bending it around the base of your loop. Trim any excess wire, and sand the wire ends with 240-grit sandpaper to dull the points.

C

D

Carved Ring

ARTIST
Joanna Gollberg

THIS SIMPLE RING IS AN EXCELLENT INTRODUCTION TO THE JOY OF FREE-FORM CARVING WITH A MOTORIZED TOOL AND BURR. THE BURR NOT ONLY MAKES THE WORK GO FASTER, IT ALLOWS YOU TO CREATE A MORE FLOWING LINE OF CARVING.

MATERIALS

Cherry wood cube, ½ x 1½ x 1½ inches
(13 x 38 x 38 mm) at each edge

Sterling silver sheet, 24 gauge*

Hard silver solder

Flux

Pickling solution

Sandpaper: 220 and 400 grit

Paste wax

Soft cloth

Steel wool, 0000 grade

*Most jewelry supply companies offer
premade ring bands that you can
use to complete this project.

TOOLS

Steel ruler, inch and millimeter

Jeweler's saw and blades

Half-round and round files

Soldering equipment

Rawhide hammer

Ring mandrel

Pencil

Flexible shaft tool and 1.5-mm drill bit

Coping saw (optional)

Drill press, Forstner bit, and
expandable pliers (optional)

Round burr, 2 mm

Split mandrel

Chasing hammer

Large dapping punch, about 1 inch
(25 mm) in diameter

Steel block

PROCESS

1. Determine your ring size to find the proper length measurement for your ring. Mark the proper length on your sheet of 24-gauge sterling silver, and mark the width of the rectangle at ⅝ inch (16 mm).

2. Cut out the silver rectangle for the ring band, using the jeweler's saw. File the short edges straight.

3. Bend the band into a circular form, making sure the edges are flush, then solder your ring band together with hard solder. Pickle the band and rinse it (photo A).

4. Use the rawhide hammer to shape the ring on your ring mandrel.

5. Sand the ring with 220- and 400-grit sandpaper to remove all scratches on the inside and outside of the band.

6. Center an edge of the band on the end grain of the block of cherry, then use a pencil to trace the circumference of the ring onto the wood. Hold the pencil so that it makes a mark exactly at the corner of the metal and wood. Do the same on the opposite side of the block (photo B).

7. Use the 1.5-mm drill bit in the flexible shaft tool to drill a hole near the inside edge of the circle. Insert the blade of the jeweler's saw or coping saw into this hole and slowly saw out the center of the block. Check your progress on the opposite face frequently. Make the hole a little smaller than the traced circle. Alternatively, you can find a Forstner bit that's slightly smaller than the circle, chuck it in a drill press, hold the block with expandable pliers, and bore the hole.

A	B

8. Using the round file, widen the hole gradually until the silver tube slides through it. Use the silver ring often to check your progress at both ends of the hole.

9. Draw another circle concentrically around the hole. This circle should be ¼ inch (6 mm) larger in diameter than the first one.

10. Using one of the saws, remove the wood around the larger circle, and trim both ends of the ring to make it exactly 12 mm tall.

11. Use the 2 mm round burr mounted on the flexible shaft tool to carve any design you like in the wood. Be patient while carving; excess wood can always be removed, but you cannot replace it later if you take too much off in the first place.

12. Use the 400-grit sandpaper in the split mandrel to sand and smooth the wood on your ring. Then give the wood a nice shine by rubbing it with the paste wax and a soft cloth.

13. Insert the silver band into the wooden ring. Leave 2 mm hanging out at each end.

14. Use the chasing hammer, the dapping punch, and the steel block to gently flare each end of the inner ring, one side at a time. Flip the ring over after each blow so you don't flare one side all at once. Flare the silver in this manner until the band will no longer flare.

15. With the ring still resting on the steel block, use the ball end of your chasing hammer to press the metal over the edges of the wooden ring. Be gentle but firm with your hammer blows.

16. Give the inside of the silver band a final finish with 0000-grade steel wool.

Bog Oak & Silver Necklace

ARTIST
Vladimir Levestam

HERE'S A CHANCE TO ADD SOME HISTORY TO YOUR JEWELRY. OAK TREES THAT FELL INTO PEAT BOGS CENTURIES AGO WERE PRESERVED BY NATURALLY ACIDIC WATER AND ANAEROBIC CONDITIONS THAT KEPT THE OAK FROM ROTTING. TANNINS IN THE BOG PRESERVED AS WELL AS DARKENED THE WOOD.

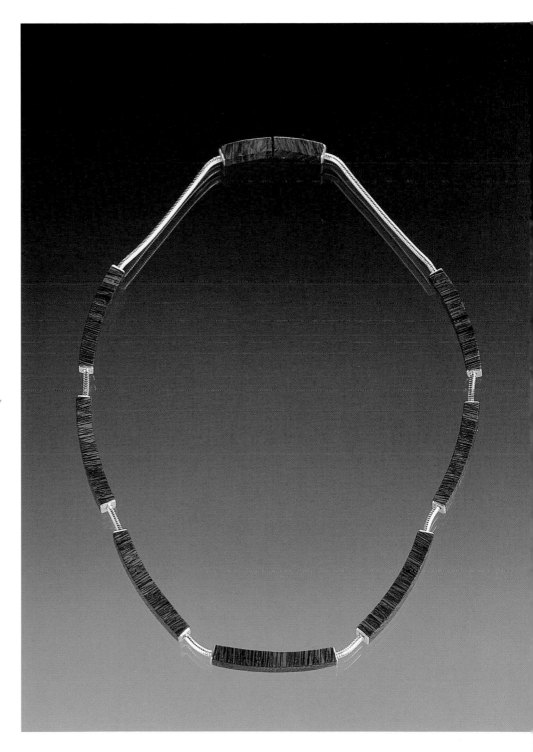

MATERIALS

Bog oak (photo A), ¼ x 1⅝ x 2 inches (6 mm x 41 mm x 51 mm)

Cardboard

Tin foil sheet, 0.3 mm x 1 inch (25 mm) square*

Cyanoacrylate glue, in gel form

Sandpaper: 220, 320, and 600 grit

2 cylindrical magnets, ³⁄₁₆ inch (5 mm) in diameter, ⅛ inch (3 mm) long

Natural wax polish (50 percent organic beeswax, 50 percent turpentine)

Polishing cloth

Silver-plated snake chain, 2 mm in diameter, 16 inches (40.6 cm) long

*The material is a tin foil sheet, not the more common and much thinner aluminum foil you have in your kitchen drawer.

TOOLS

Pencil compass

Steel ruler, inch and millimeter

Scissors

Coping saw

Drill, with 2- and 4-mm bits

Wire cutters

PROCESS

1. Use the pencil compass to draw two concentric arcs on the cardboard, with radii of 5½ and 5¾ inches (145 and 150 mm). Using the ruler, mark a radius through the two arcs and another one 1½ inches (38 mm) from the first, measured along the larger arc. The area enclosed by those four lines is the pattern for the wooden elements of the necklace. Cut out the pattern.

2. Trace the pattern eight times onto the bog oak, with the length of the pattern matching the grain direction in the oak (photo A). Use the coping saw to cut out the shape (photo B).

3. Using the ruler and pencil, mark 16 squares, each ¼ inch (6 mm) on a side, on the tinfoil. Cut out the tin squares with the scissors.

4. Mix a small batch of the cyanoacrylate glue, and affix tin squares to the ends of the eight arcs of oak.

5. Sand the wooden pieces with 220-grit sandpaper. When you've removed all the saw marks, sand the pieces to a finer finish with 320- and 600-grit

sandpaper. Leave the edges sharp.

6. Using the drill and the 2-mm drill bit, drill holes ⁷⁄₁₆ inch (10 mm) deep in each butt end of every wooden piece (photo C).

7. Cut one of the oak pieces in half to serve as bases for the two magnetic clasps.

8. Use the drill and the 4-mm bit to bore holes ⅛ inch (3 mm) deep in the newly cut ends.

9. Mix a little more cyanoacrylate glue, and glue the magnets into the holes (photo D). Sand the magnet ends with the 600-grit sandpaper.

10. Put some natural wax polish on a piece of soft cloth, and polish all nine wooden pieces.

11. Use the wire cutters to cut the snake chain into six 11¾-inch (30 mm) pieces and two 3¼-inch (80 mm) pieces. Put the clasp parts aside. Glue a short chain between each pair of oak arcs, arranging them so that the concave sides face inward. Finally, glue the long chains between the remaining arc ends.

Natural Wax Polish

To make the natural wax polish yourself, combine equal parts of organic beeswax and oil of turpentine. Melt them gently over a water bath, and stir. Pour the mixture into a glass jar, and allow it to cool. Victorian recipes call for white soap flakes, vinegar, and ethyl alcohol to be added while the mixture is liquid. Try these additives at your own risk.

A

B

C

D

Brooch with Holes

ARTIST

Marjorie Schick

A CLASSIC

DEMILUNE SHAPE

BECOMES A

CANVAS FOR A

SINGULAR, ARTISTIC

EXPRESSION IN

THIS WORTH-A-

SECOND-LOOK

BROOCH.

MATERIALS

2 pieces of birch plywood, each ⅛ inch (3 mm) thick and at least 3½ x 8½ inches (89 x 216 mm)

Double-stick tape

Sandpaper, 220 grit

Stainless steel wire, 18 gauge

Wood glue

Waxed paper

Emery paper: 320, 400, 500, and 600 grit

Wood filler

Acrylic gesso

Acrylic paints

TOOLS

Pencil

Steel ruler

Handsaw

Coping saw

Drill

Drill bits: ⁷⁄₃₂ inch (6 mm), ⁵⁄₁₆ inch (8 mm), ³⁄₈ inch (10 mm), and #56

Jeweler's saw and #4 saw blades

Band saw (optional)

Needle files, round and half-round

Dowels (for sandpaper)

8-inch (20.3 cm) round file

Wire cutters

Vise

Mallet

Craft knife

Flexible shaft tool and wheel burr (optional)

C-clamps

Round-nose pliers

Artist brushes

PROCESS

1. Draw the shape for the brooch in the desired size onto one piece of the ⅛-inch-thick (3 mm) birch plywood. The brooch shown here is 3⅛ x 8¼ inches (7.9 x 21 cm). To cut matching pieces, first fasten the two plywood pieces together with a strip of double-stick tape between the layers. Then cut both shapes at once, using the handsaw and coping saw.

2. Plan a design for the holes. To provide variety to her brooch, the designer used three different drill bits—⁷⁄₃₂ inch (6 mm), ⁵⁄₁₆ inch (8 mm), and ³⁄₈ inch (10 mm). Drill most of the holes through only the top piece of plywood, although several can go through both pieces so that the color of the wearer's shirt will show through (photo A on the next page). Cut lines into the brooch with a jeweler's saw with a large blade such as a #4, or with a band saw.

3. Using round files and/or sandpaper wrapped around a dowel, bevel the sides of some holes.

4. Plan the placement of the pin and hook. Because of the size and weight of this brooch, use two vertical pins rather than a single pin stem. On the front side of the back piece, draw two vertical lines representing the path of the pin wires. Make sure that these lines are not visible through the holes of the front piece. The lines should stop about ³⁄₈ inch (10 mm) from the edges of the brooch, where the holes for the pin wire will go (photo B on the next page).

A

B

5. To begin making the pins, use the wire cutters to cut two pieces of the 18-gauge stainless steel wire. Their lengths should be about 2½ times the distance between the hole marks.

6. Making sure that you have enough wire on one end for the pin and on the other for the hook, make two sharp, right-angle bends in each piece of wire. Bend the wire by gripping it in the vise, starting the bend by hand, and finishing it with a mallet, striking down on the top of the vise jaws. The bent ends should be parallel (photo C).

7. To be certain that the holes for the pin wire are the correct distance apart, drill test holes through scrap plywood to get the exact placement before drilling into the brooch. It's likely your pins will not be exactly the same. Use the #56 drill bit to make four holes in the back piece.

8. Use a sharp craft knife or a wheel burr in a flexible shaft tool to make a groove along the marked lines between each pair of holes. Since it will hold the pin wire and allow the front and back to be glued together, the groove should be just deep enough to contain the wire and no deeper.

9. Push the pin wires through the holes and seat them in their grooves (photo D). Spread wood glue on the pieces of plywood, match their edges, and press them together. Cover the outer surfaces with waxed paper to prevent anything else from sticking to the brooch. Clamp the two pieces of plywood firmly, using C-clamps pushing on scrap wood clamping pads. Make sure that you have enough clamps to squeeze glue out all around the edges.

10. Allow the wood glue to cure for at least one hour. Using round-nose pliers, bend the pin stem and hook into position, providing ⅛-inch (3 mm) clearance between the pin and the wood back.

11. Cut the hook to length, then file and sand the end with emery paper to make it smooth. Cut the end of the pin stem, making certain that it extends far enough beyond the hook. File the end of the pin either to a taper or to a blunt tip, then sand it with progressively finer emery paper, up to 600 grit.

12. Sand the edges of the brooch, and apply wood filler as necessary. Sand a final time with 220-grit sandpaper.

13. Gesso the front and back of the brooch. When the gesso is dry, paint the brooch with acrylic paint, or decorate it in any other way you desire.

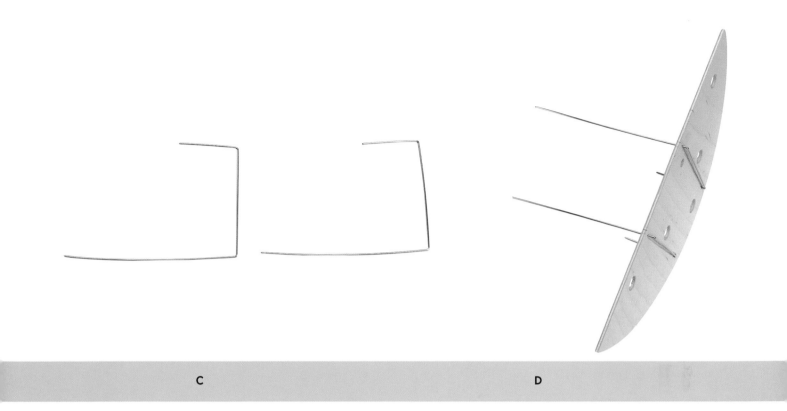

C

D

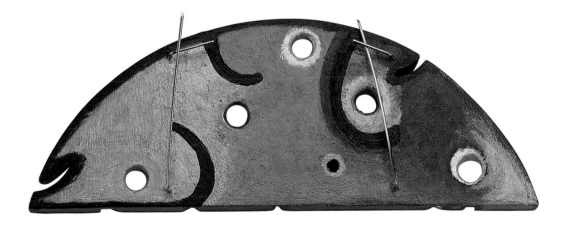

Finished brooch back

Boxwood Pendant & Earrings

ARTIST

Monique Escoulen

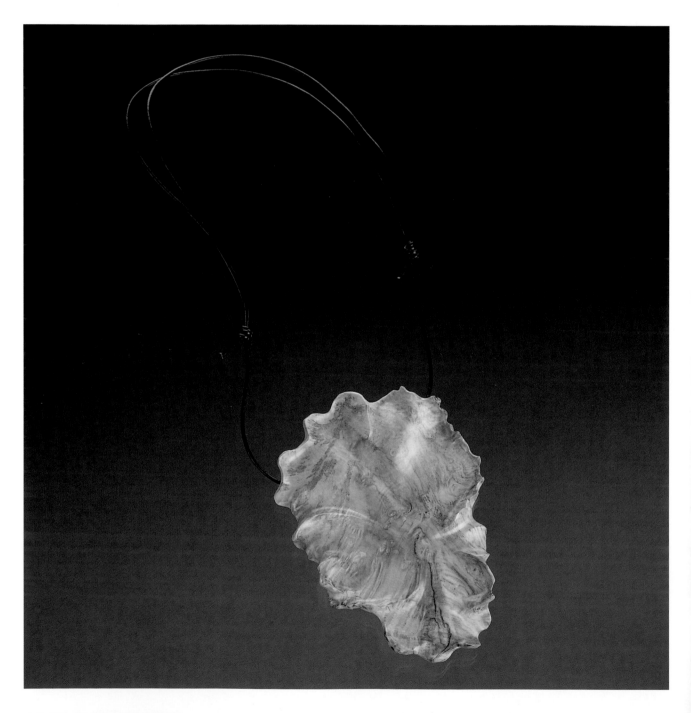

ROOTS AND BURLS ARE BELOVED BY WOOD

AFICIONADOS—THE INTRICATE GRAINING

AND COLOR ARE VISUAL DELIGHTS. JEWELRY

CREATED WITH THIS TYPE OF WOOD NEEDS

LITTLE EMBELLISHMENT OR ENHANCEMENT.

MATERIALS

Boxwood root

Hot-glue stick

Sandpaper: 180, 240, and 320 grit

2 short sterling silver wires

Satin cellulose shellac and thinner

Leather lacing, 30 inches (76 cm)

Cyanoacrylate glue

Double-stick tape

2 ring rods

Sterling silver earwires

TOOLS

Band saw

Bar clamp (optional)

Router and router planing jig

Hot-glue gun

Random orbit sander

Awl

Drill, with 0.8- and 1-mm drill bits

Flexible shaft tool, with rasps and
burrs, and sanding roll

Magnifying glass

Airbrush or small, high-quality
paintbrush

Coping saw

Knife

Needle-nose pliers

A

PROCESS

Pendant

1. Select a boxwood root, keeping in mind the size of the pendant you want to make. Examine the shape of the root to find its most interesting areas. Remember that the pendant and earrings have rough edges from the outside of the root (photo A).

2. Using the band saw, cut through the root once and then again to produce a ⅜-inch-thick (10 mm) slice. Make sure that part of the root rests on the saw table, under or very close to where you're sawing. If the wood being sawn hangs in midair, the blade can catch and jerk the root down to the table, damaging the root, the saw, or you—or any combination thereof. If you anticipate having trouble holding the root, tighten a bar clamp to the root where the clamp won't be in the way. Position the bar clamp so that it lays flat on the saw table.

You can't draw guidelines for the cut, so you must visualize the path of the saw. If you cut a ball root perpendicular to the axis, you get a round piece; if you cut it obliquely, you get a nearly oval shape.

3. With the router and the router planing jig described on page 63, plane the pendant's back face. It's not necessary to plane the front face before carving it.

4. Decide where to drill the hole or holes for the leather lacing. For a large pendant, drill two holes, one on each side, near the top of the pendant. You can drill one hole from edge to edge on a small pendant. Mark the hole locations with an awl, and use the drill and 1-mm drill bit to drill a ⅝-inch-deep (16 mm) hole into each edge. These holes should be parallel with the back surface.

5. Now you're ready to carve. Use the flexible shaft tool with rasps and burrs. Begin with a rasp to take off wood quickly and reveal the main lines of your design. Then work with a burr. (The

designer used an olive-shaped burr.) Remember where you drilled holes and avoid carving into them.

Accentuate the lines to make the carving come alive. Work the edges at little, making them soft so they won't irritate your skin when you wear the pendant.

6. Sand the carving with the small sanding roll on the flexible shaft tool. A sanding roll consists of a small metal rod with a slit running into the end of the rod. Insert a small piece of 180-grit sandpaper into the slit to make a tiny flap sander. Change the sandpaper often, and avoid deforming your carved surface.

7. Get rid of all imperfections with the 180-grit paper. Then sand with 240 grit and 320 grit. Check the results with the magnifying glass.

8. Use a good-quality satin cellulose shellac to finish the pendant. For the first coat, use a half-and-half mixture of shellac and thinner. The designer used an airbrush to spray the shellac evenly, keeping the nozzle about 3 inches (76 mm) away from the surface. Coat all surfaces of the pendant, and let it dry for 30 minutes. You can also apply the shellac with a small, high-quality brush, but work quickly to stay ahead of the rapidly drying shellac.

9. Carefully check the surfaces again to determine whether more sanding is necessary. For the second coat, use a mixture of three parts shellac to one part thinner.

10. When the shellac is dry, glue the leather lacing ends into the holes using cyanoacrylate glue. Take care to put enough glue in the hole bottom. Cut the lacing at its middle and tie slip knots at the ends.

Earrings

11. Twin earrings present two problems: matching the wood and carving mirror-image forms. You can match the wood by finding two pieces with similar color and grain, by cutting two successive slices from a root and opening them like a book (book-matching), or by cutting a large slice in half.

12. Plane the two pieces of wood with the router, and sand their back faces with 180-, 240-, and 320-grit sandpaper. Attach their back faces together with double-stick tape so that you can work on both earrings at once.

13. Draw and cut their exterior shape with the band saw or coping saw.

14. Carve them with the flexible shaft tool, going back and forth from face to face, building the same forms, but reversed on the two faces. This will seem very natural if the shape of the earrings is asymmetrical.

15. Shape the edges and use the sharp knife to cut a small, flat place on the top for the rod rings.

16. Sand the faces and edges with 180-grit sandpaper, followed 240 and 320 grit. Separate the two pieces by prying them apart with a knife.

17. With the 0.8-mm drill bit, bore a ⅜-inch-deep (10 mm) hole at each of the flattened parts of the edges.

18. Use the short sterling silver wires to create two wire loops. Use cyanoacrylate glue to secure the loops in the holes.

19. Finish the earrings with shellac, just as you finished the pendant.

20. When the two coats of shellac are dry, use needle-nose pliers to hang the silver ear loops from.

Router Thickness Planer

Here's an excellent method, suggested by Monique Escoulen for thickness planing small pieces of wood. Of course, it only works if you own a router.

Begin with a piece of MDF (Medium Density Fiberboard) or good-quality plywood, ¾ inch (19 mm) thick and about 12 inches (30 cm) square. Cut two strips of the same material, about 1¼ inches (32 mm) wide and 12 inches (30 cm) long. Fasten the strips to opposite edges of the square with wood glue and three screws per strip. Drive the screws through the square and into the strips.

Prepare the router by fastening to its base a ½-inch-thick (13 mm) or ¾-inch-thick (19 mm) piece of MDF or plywood that's at least 24 inches (61 cm) long and the width of the router base. When using this fixture, clamp it to a bench, and keep the extended router base perpendicular to the base strips. Use paste wax to lubricate the top surfaces of the strips and the bottom of the extended router base.

Fasten your workpiece to the base with one bead of hot glue that runs the length of the wood. Make sure the glue gun is preheated before you start, and press the piece of wood down firmly while the glue is still hot.

Use a ¾-inch (19 mm) plunge-cutting straight bit in the router. Adjust its height to remove ¹⁄₁₆ inch (1.6 mm) of wood at a time, and slide the router over the entire surface of the work piece. Lower the cutter until the surface is smooth and flat.

While the wood is attached to the base, do any machine sanding necessary. Use a chisel to pry the wood piece away from the base. If it doesn't lift easily, or if you're worried about breaking the wood, use a hair dryer to heat the wood until the glue softens.

Flip the wood, and plane the other side to give it an even thickness.

Pinto Earrings

ARTIST
Mayra Orama Muniz

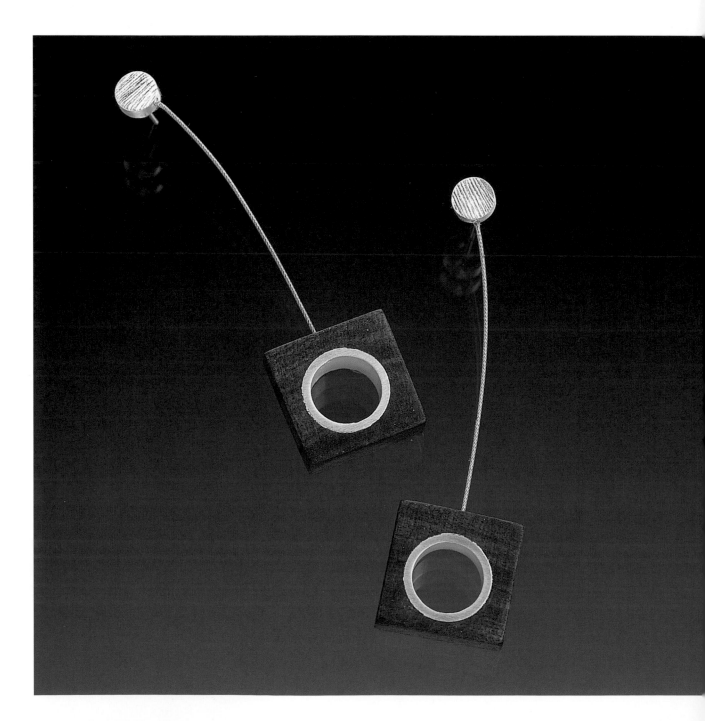

JUST A SPLASH
OF ROBIN'S EGG
BLUE GIVES A
PLAYFUL TOUCH
TO THESE
GEOMETRIC
EARRINGS.

MATERIALS

Redheart wood, at least ¾ inch (19 mm) thick

Aluminum round tube, ½ inch (13 mm) outside diameter

Sandpaper: 120, 150, 220, and 320 grit

Enamel paint

Aluminum rod, ¼ inch (6 mm) in diameter

Flexible stainless-steel cable

Aluminum wire, 19 gauge

Earring posts, 6 mm, with backs

Epoxy, two part five-minute

Oil finish

Cotton rags

Steel wool, 0000 grade

TOOLS

6-inch (15.2 cm) ruler

Band saw

Bench belt sander, with 120- and 220-grit belts

Drill press with ½-inch (13 mm) drill bit

Hacksaw or metal-cutting band saw

Mallet

Small paintbrush

Engineer's square

Center punch

Self-locking pliers

#61 drill bit

File

Wire cutters

Flat-nose pliers

Artist brushes

PROCESS

1. Use the band saw to cut a ¾-inch (19 mm) cube of redheart a little oversize (photo A).

2. Sand the blank to a true ¾-inch (19 mm) cube, using the bench belt sander with the 120-grit belt.

3. Mark the center of the cube's long-grain face. Use the drill press and ½-inch (13 mm) bit to bore a hole through the center of the cube (photo B).

A

B

C

4. Cut a $\frac{13}{16}$-inch-long (21 mm) piece of the round aluminum tube, using the hacksaw or metal-cutting band saw. Make sure that the tube is slightly longer than the hole in the blank. You can file and sand it flush with the wood later (photo C).

5. Press the tube into the hole. Tap it with the mallet if necessary.

6. Use the hacksaw or the metal-cutting band saw to cut the cube (across the tube) into two squares of equal thickness.

7. Use the belt sander and 120-grit belt to smooth the sawn faces. Keep the faces flat and parallel with the opposite faces. Then switch to the 220-grit belt, and sand all the faces lightly to remove the 120-grit scratches while keeping the faces flat. Spread the 320-grit sandpaper on a smooth, flat surface and sand all the faces again by moving the squares across the paper, with the grain, of course. Photo C shows the ends of aluminum tubes before and after sanding.

8. Paint the insides of the tubes with the enamel paint. The designer used a robin's egg blue.

9. With the hacksaw or metal-cutting band saw, cut two ⅛-inch-long (3 mm) pieces from the aluminum rod. File the faces flat and square to the edges.

10. Mark the center of a long-grain edge of each square, and deepen each mark with the center punch. Punch a dimple on the edge of each aluminum disc. Hold the pieces with self-locking pliers while you drill holes with the #61 drill bit. Drill through a wall of the aluminum tube in the squares and halfway through the discs.

11. With the wire cutters, cut two 2-inch-long (51 mm) pieces of the flexible stainless steel cable.

12. Cut four 1-inch-long (25 mm) pieces of the 19 gauge aluminum wire, and file one end of each to a point. Trim two points to fit inside the aluminum tube.

13. Use an aluminum wire piece to wedge the cable into the hole from the inside of each tube. Push a cable end through a hole, and press the wire point into the hole with the flat-nose pliers. Cut and file off the excess cable and point.

14. Wedge the aluminum discs on the other ends of the cables, using the same method.

15. Using the epoxy, glue the 6 mm earring post backs onto the aluminum discs.

16. When the glue cures, finish the wood, using any method described on page 24.

Make yourself an extra earring to create a matching pendant. Shorten the length of cable used, omit the earring posts, and drill a hole through the aluminum rod.

Measure Twice,
Cut Once Necklace

ARTIST

Cyndi Lavin

WORDS AND IMAGES PERTAINING TO WOOD FROM VINTAGE DICTIONARIES EMBELLISH A REVERSIBLE NECKLACE CREATED WITH RULERS AND YARDSTICKS. YOU'LL BE ABLE TO MEASURE PEOPLE'S REACTIONS WHEN YOU WEAR IT.

MATERIALS

Vintage rulers and yardsticks (photo A)

Brass or gold-toned lanyard hooks

Sandpaper, 120 and 180 grit

Old dictionaries or other wood-related texts (photo B)

Water-soluble oil pastels

Decoupage medium

Vintage brass or gold-toned chain, 25 inches (63.5 cm) long

Brass or gold-toned jump rings, 7 mm

TOOLS

Handsaw or power miter saw

Drill and $\frac{5}{64}$-inch (2 mm) drill bit or a size to accommodate the lanyard hook

Sanding block (optional)

Craft knife

Small paintbrushes

Flat-nose pliers

Decorative-edge scissors (optional)

PROCESS

1. Remove any brass or metal edges from the rulers. Using the handsaw or power miter saw, cut the rulers and yardsticks into pieces. (Wear safety glasses if you use the miter saw.) Cutting a variety of sizes will allow you to create a graduated look on the finished necklace.

2. Decide in which direction you want each of your ruler pieces to be oriented, then drill a $\frac{5}{64}$-inch (2 mm) hole in the upper corner of each one. Old rulers and yardsticks can be dried out, delicate, and prone to cracking, so drill carefully. After drilling the first hole, check to make sure that a lanyard hook will fit through it.

3. Clean up the sawn ends with 120-grit sandpaper followed by 180-grit paper. Use a sanding block for this step, or place the sandpaper, grit side up, on your work surface.

4. Cut or tear out words and images from old dictionaries or other texts about wood. Use the decorative-edge

A

A GOOD RULE "Do Unto Others As You Would Have Them Do Unto You"

scissors to trim each one to fit a ruler or yardstick piece. Save one of the smallest pieces to use as a dangle at the end of the chain.

5. Using water-soluble oil pastels, color an irregular spot on the back of each wood piece, large enough to be seen around the edges of the text or image you've chosen for that piece. Color the sanded edges of the ruler if desired.

6. Using a small paintbrush, apply a thin coat of decoupage medium to the back of a ruler piece. Apply the text or image for that piece and smooth it into place. You should be able to wipe small amounts of tint onto the paper, as your brush will pick up some of the pastel. Clean your brushes frequently to avoid mixing colors.

7. When you have applied all the text and images, brush another thin coat of decoupage medium over the entire back of each one and over its painted ends. Don't allow any glaze to dribble onto the front of the pieces. Let all the pieces dry thoroughly.

8. Slip each ruler or yardstick piece onto a lanyard hook, helping it along with the flat-nose pliers if necessary. Spread out the chain. Place the smallest cut piece at one end of the chain, ruler side down, then lay out the other cut pieces in the order you want them in the necklace, also ruler side down. Starting from the middle and working outward, attach each hook to the chain with a 7 mm jump ring. Attach the smallest piece to one end of the chain with a lanyard hook, and attach the leftover lanyard hook to the other end as a clasp.

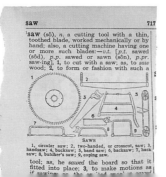

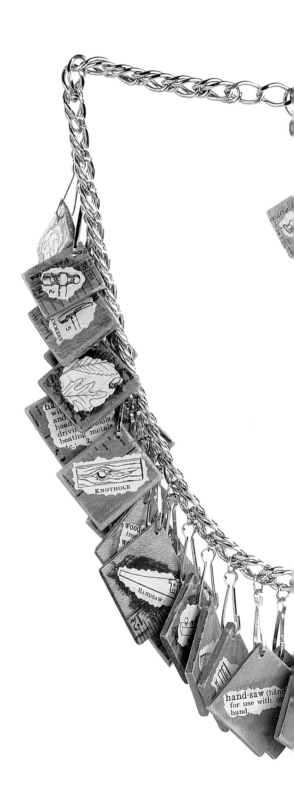

Sterling Silver & Purpleheart Earrings

MATERIALS

Purpleheart wood, ½ inch (13 mm)
  thick (photo A on the next page)

Dead soft sterling silver sheet,
  20 gauge

Sterling silver wire, 16 and 18 gauge

Drawing paper

Tracing paper

Cardboard

Sandpaper for wood: 120, 180, and
  240 grit

Dowels in different diameters
  (optional)

Masking tape (optional)

Solder, medium or easy

Flux

Pickling solution

Earring posts and backs, silver or gold

Wet-or-dry sandpaper: 320 and
  600 grit

Steel wool, 0000 grade (optional)

Green kitchen scrubbing pad
  (optional)

Cyanoacrylate glue or two-part
  five-minute epoxy

Shop rag or paper towels

Oil finish

Cotton rags

TOOLS

Steel ruler, inch and millimeter

Pencil

Scissors or craft knife

Fine-tipped permanent marker or
  scratch awl

Jeweler's saw, with #2/0 and
  #8 blades

Band saw or coping saw (both
  optional)

Fine rasp

Flat or half-round coarse and fine
  files, 6 or 8 inches (15.2 or 20.3 cm)

Flexible shaft tool, with cylinder or
  oval burr

Half-round, barrette, and fish-belly
  coarse needle files, medium cut

Round-nose pliers

Wire cutters

Soldering equipment

Drill and 1 mm drill bit

PURPLEHEART—GROWN IN CENTRAL AND SOUTH

AMERICA—IS A FAVORITE OF WOODWORKERS

WORLDWIDE. THE HEARTWOOD PRODUCES THE

PURPLE SHADES THAT LOOK SO BEAUTIFUL WHEN

PAIRED WITH SILVER.

A	B	C	D

PROCESS

1. Draw your earring designs on drawing paper, then trace the designs onto tracing paper (or just draw on the tracing paper). Transfer your designs to a piece of cardboard. Using the scissors or craft knife, cut the traced shapes accurately to use as templates.

2. Using the very fine-tipped permanent marker or scratch awl, trace your shapes on the purpleheart and on the 20-gauge sterling silver sheet. Cutting just outside the traced lines, cut out the metal with the #2/0 blade in the jeweler's saw and cut out the wood with the thicker #8 blade (photo B). You can cut the wood with a band saw or a coping saw if you like.

3. Use the rasp and coarse files to reduce the wooden piece to your cutting line. Start carving the wood by knocking down the corners of the sharp edges, deciding where you want the surfaces to curve in or out. Animate flat planes by making them wave or twist; try to find how the shape wants to turn into a three-dimensional form (photo C).

4. When the forms are close to what you want, start smoothing and refining them with the smaller, finer files and then with 120-grit sandpaper. After removing all tool marks with the 120-grit paper, remove the sanding scratches with 180-grit and 240-grit sandpaper.

5. Shape the silver parts the same way as the wood parts. Smooth the edges

using medium files, then switch to fine files to finish smoothing and to remove any burr edges that have appeared. Using a light touch, curve the metal shapes with your fingers. Slight curves often produce a big visual effect (photo D). Use dowels or other curved surfaces to help bend the metal evenly. If you must use pliers, pad the jaws with several layers of masking tape.

6. Use the round-nose pliers to make two tiny jump rings from the 18-gauge silver wire, each large enough to fit around the 16-gauge wire. Solder an earring post to the back of each silver piece. Decide how you want the earrings to hang, and solder each jump ring to the edge of a silver piece, at a point directly below the pin (photo E).

7. Finish the silver parts by wet sanding the edges with 320- and 600-grit wet-or-dry sandpaper. Texture the faces of the silver with the 600-grit paper, the 0000-grade steel wool, or the green kitchen scrubbing pad.

8. Drill a 1 mm hole, ¼ inch (6 mm) deep, at the top of each wood piece. Use the round-nose pliers to make a tiny loop in the end of a piece of 16-gauge wire, slipping the jump ring of an earring into the loop before you close it. Use the wire cutters to cut the wire ¼ inch (6 mm) from the loop. Make another loop for the second earring. Make sure that the pins fit into the holes properly; the loops should touch the wood. Put a little cyanoacrylate glue or epoxy into the holes, and dip the end of each wire into the glue before pushing the wires into the holes. Use a shop rag or paper towel to wipe up any excess glue before it cures (photo E).

9. Use oil finish to darken and shine the purpleheart. Follow the manufacturer's instructions or those on page 24.

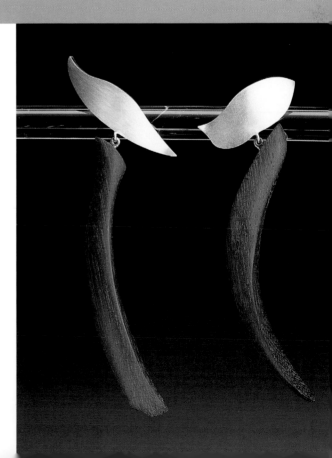

Twig Suite

ARTIST
Cynthia
B. Wuller

IT'S HARD TO IMPROVE UPON THE NATURAL BEAUTY OF DELICATE TWIGS—UNLESS YOU EMBELLISH THEM WITH THE SPRING-LIKE GREEN OF PERIDOT BEADS.

MATERIALS

2 thin red dogwood twigs, each 2 inches (51 mm) long, preferably tips with buds*

Wishbone-shaped red dogwood twig, 3 inches (76 mm) long (photo A)*

Copper wire, 24 gauge

2 peridot beads, 3 mm

2 copper or gold ear hooks

2 green garnet beads, 5 mm

Copper chain, 16 inches (45 cm) long

Copper hook-and-eye clasp

*Any species of twig will work for these earrings, but the designer prefers the warm color of red dogwood. You can gather your own twigs or buy them from craft stores or florist shops. These twigs are delicate and must be handled carefully to avoid marring the bark.

TOOLS

Steel ruler

Wire cutters

Knife

Chain-nose pliers

Straight sewing pin

Round-nose pliers

Chasing hammer

Bench block

A

PROCESS

Earrings

1. Use the wire cutters to cut two pieces of the 24-gauge wire, each 4 inches (102 mm) long, and two pieces, each 3 inches (76 mm) long. Use a sharp knife or wire cutters to trim the twigs to the desired sizes, leaving the buds on the twigs.

2. With the chain-nose pliers, make a right-angle bend 1¼ inches (32 mm) from one end of each 4-inch-long (102 mm) wire. Using the straight pin, poke a hole ¼ inch (6 mm) from the trimmed end of a twig (photo B). Slide the long part of one bent wire through the hole until the short end rests against the twig. With one jaw of the round-nose pliers held against the end of the twig to serve as a guide, bend the wire over the pliers and back toward the hole on the other side of the twig. The loop should be ⅛ inch (3 mm) tall. Pinch the loop with the chain-nose pliers so the wire lies tight along the twig.

3. Wrap the long end of the wire around the loop wire and the twig (photo C).

Wind a tight coil to the trimmed end, making sure that the loop doesn't twist. Cut the coil end at the end of the twig, and secure it by gently pinching the wire into the twig with the chain-nose pliers.

4. Trim the short end of loop wire at the coil and pull up on the loop slightly with chain-nose pliers to hide the end under the coil. Gently hammer the loop on the bench block to harden it. Repeat these steps with the other twig.

5. Form a "U" shape, sized to fit the twig, in a 3-inch-long (76 mm) wire, about ¾ inch (19 mm) from one end. Wrap the short end twice around the twig, about ¾ inch (19 mm) down from the bud. Slip a bead onto the wire, and lay the bead flat against the twig, at an angle (photo D). Wrap the wire two times around the twig to secure the bead. Trim the excess wire on the side of the twig opposite the bead. With the chain-nose pliers, gently pinch the wire ends to the twig. Repeat this process with the other twig, but attach the bead ¾ inch (19 mm) from the loop end.

6. Finally, attach the ear hooks.

Pendant

7. Cut one 5-inch (125 mm) piece and two 3½-inch (88 mm) pieces of wire. Use a sharp knife or wire cutters to clip the ends of the wishbone-shaped twig at sharp angles for a better visual flow. The designer left one end a little shorter than the other. Trim the main twig straight across.

8. Repeat steps 2 to 4 to form a wire loop on the fat end of the wishbone.

9. Decide where to attach your beads. The designer placed hers ¾ inch (19 mm) from the end of the longer wishbone leg and 1 inch (25 mm) from the top of the other leg. She also varied their appearance by using three wraps on each side of the lower bead and two wraps for the other.

10. Attach the beads using the process described in step 5.

11. Slip the chain through the loop of the pendant, and attach the hook and eye clasp.

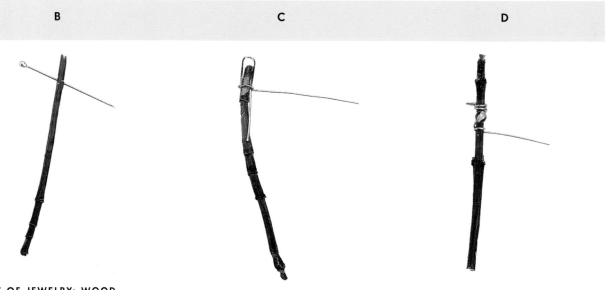

B   C   D

Pyrography-Patterned Brooches

ARTIST
Carolyn
A. Currin

FORGET THOSE SUMMER CAMP EXPERIENCES WITH A WOOD-BURNING

TOOL. THESE BROOCHES ILLUSTRATE THAT EVEN THE DOWDIEST OF

CRAFT TECHNIQUES CAN BE USED FOR GREAT EFFECTS.

MATERIALS

Craft plywood, ⅛ inch (3 mm) thick

Paste wax

Soft cloth

Copper sheet, 22 or 20 gauge

Masking tape

Medium solder

Flux

Pin back

Pickling solution

Liver of Sulfur solution

TOOLS

Pencil

Flexible shaft tool or small, handheld
rotary tool

Drill bit, any size from .96 mm to
1.18 mm

Jeweler's saw and blades (coarse
and fine)

Half-round file

Wood-burning tool with
decorative tips

Flat-nose pliers

Fine-tipped permanent marker

Bench pin

Steel block or anvil

Chasing tools (optional)

Chasing hammer (optional)

Oxygen-acetylene torch

Copper tongs

Brass brush

Tweezers

PROCESS

1. After choosing a shape for your pyrography brooch, use the pencil to draw it onto the craft plywood. Use the flexible shaft tool or small, handheld rotary tool and the drill bit to drill a hole within the inner circle. Thread a coarse-tooth blade through the hole, and attach it to the jeweler's saw frame. Cut the inner circle and then the outer shape. File the outer edge smooth, rounding the edges as you do (photo A).

2. Attach an ornamental-pattern tip to the wood-burning tool, and let it warm up. Use a scrap of the plywood to practice working with the tool. Take some time to learn how it works, and play with different tips. Once you're comfortable with the process, burn the surface design on your wood shape. If you're using more than one tip shape, use pliers to change the tip. When you're finished, apply two or three coats of paste wax to enhance the natural color of the wood. Rub the wax with the soft cotton cloth to shine it. Remove any excess wax.

3. To create the copper backing, use the pencil to trace the shape of the plywood front onto the copper sheet. Using the fine-point permanent marker, make the pencil lines darker, and draw the tabs that will hold the copper and plywood together. The tabs will be visible on the finished brooch, so consider their placement carefully. Draw both inner and

A	B

outer tabs, making them long enough to bend around to the front of the plywood. Working on the bench pin, cut the backing shape using the jeweler's saw. With the half-round file, smooth the edges and tabs, rounding the ends of the tabs to lessen the chance of catching a blouse or sweater on them (photo B).

4. If you desire chased designs on the back of your copper backing, add them now. Figure out which side of the copper backing is the back, and set it on the steel block or anvil, with the back facing up. To secure the piece on the block, you can use masking tape. Chase your design with the chasing tools (any kind you prefer) and chasing hammer (photo C).

5. Before you solder the pin back to the copper, decide where the top of your brooch should be. (If you haven't soldered before, read the detailed instructions on page 26.) Working on the firebrick or another safe surface, use the oxygen-acetylene torch and medium solder to solder the pin back. Quench the copper backing in water and put it in the pickling solution.

6. Using copper tongs, remove the copper backing from the pickling solution and rinse it in water. Clean the copper with the sponge, dish soap, and warm water. Then drop it into the Liver of Sulfur solution, and leave it until you see the color you want. Using the copper tongs again, remove the patinated cop-

per backing, and rinse it with water. Finish the copper backing by scrubbing it under warm water with the brass brush.

7. Hold the wood-burned plywood on top of the copper back, and slowly bend the tabs over onto the wood piece. You can do this using a pair of flat-nose pliers with masking-tape cushions on its tips to protect the copper from scratches. Try to turn the prong tips into the plywood so that they hold the front securely and present a finished face.

C

Laminated Wood Earrings

ARTIST
Constance Daly

IF YOU'RE LOOKING
FOR A WAY TO
COMBINE DIFFERENT
WOOD COLORS
IN ONE PIECE,
LAMINATION MAY
BE THE TECHNIQUE
YOU'RE SEARCHING
FOR. THE POSSIBILITIES
FOR CREATING
PATTERNS ARE
ENDLESS.

MATERIALS

A variety of wood pieces in contrasting colors and widths

Waxed paper

Wood glue

Shop rag or paper towel

Sandpaper: 120, 180, 220, and 320 grit

Paper or manufactured templates

Varnish, shellac, oil finish, or paste wax

Jump rings

Ear wires

Wooden and/or metal beads (optional)

TOOLS

Steel ruler

Table saw

Small bar clamps

Flux brush

Power sander (optional)

Sanding block

Router (optional)

Pencil

Band saw or coping saw

Drill with 1/16-inch (1.5 mm) bit

Needle-nose pliers

PROCESS

1. Gather a bunch of scrap wood (photo A). You might want to rip (cut with the grain) some strips immediately, using the table saw with a zero tolerance throat plate and a push stick (page 18). You're cutting the strips to the beginning thickness, not width. The thickness of the raw wood should be about 1/8 inch (3 mm) thicker than your final earrings; 1/4 to 5/16 inch (6 to 8 mm) is a good starting thickness. Sanding will reduce it to the final thickness.

Working Tip

If you keep the pieces moving as they pass the saw blade, you should be able to avoid scorching them. Scorched wood doesn't glue well. (If they always burn, get your blade sharpened.)

A

2. Arrange and rearrange the pieces to look for pleasing patterns (photo B). Varying the colors and widths of the wood can result in some dramatic contrasts. If some of the strips are too wide, rip them to width on the table saw. For the circular earrings, the designer used only long, straight pieces.

3. Once you've settled on a pattern, cut the strips to similar lengths. Make sure that the surfaces to be glued are smooth and clean.

4. Set up the clamps and practice clamping the pieces together without glue to find a good clamping strategy. Waxed flat scraps of wood clamped across the top and bottom of the lamination can help hold all the pieces flat.

5. Place a layer of waxed paper on your work surface to avoid gluing your wood to the table. Arrange the strips again, then turn each one on edge, and squeeze them together so that only the gluing edges are up. With the top edges even, use the flux brush to apply a thin layer of wood glue to the edges. Separate the strips, and position them back in order and laid flat. Press the pieces together, and apply the clamps. If a very small amount of glue squeezes out at every seam, it means that you applied the right amount of glue. If you applied too much, just wipe most of it away with paper towels.

6. Allow the glue to cure, with the clamps still in place. In comfortable temperatures, curing will take about an hour. You can leave the clamps on longer than that if you like.

7. Remove the clamps, and sand the top and bottom surfaces of the laminate. This is easiest with a power sander with 120-grit (or rougher) sandpaper, but it can be done by hand. When sanding by hand, be sure to use a sanding block. If the surfaces are very uneven, consider using the router planing method described on page 63. Take the least amount possible off one surface, then flip the lamination and do the same on the other side. When the faces are smooth, move through the finer grits, removing the previous paper's scratches completely before switching to the next finer sandpaper.

8. The previous steps explained how to create a flat block of laminate. You can begin designing the final shape of the earrings as shown on the right side of the project photo on page 80. For more complex patterns, you will need to create a complex lamination. To do this, cut the flat block of laminate at angles, arranging the pieces to create a new pattern, and then gluing the new strips together to make a second and third-generation patterns (photo C). When a pattern pleases you, draw directly on the

wood or a photocopy of your laminate (photo D). Then cut a paper pattern, and trace it twice onto the wood. If you change your mind, simply erase the lines and draw again. You can also use manufactured templates.

9. Cut the final shapes, using the band saw or coping saw. Sand the edges smooth with sandpaper wound around the sanding block. Again, begin with 120 grit and work your way up to 320 grit.

10. Drill ¹⁄₁₆-inch (1.5 mm) holes for the jump rings through the lamination near the top.

11. Apply any finish you like. Varnish, shellac, oil finish, and paste wax all work well. Follow the manufacturer's instructions.

12. Use the needle-nose pliers to open the jump rings. Run them through the holes in the cut shapes, and then close them again.

13. Insert the ear wires into the jump rings, and add one or two beads to each if you desire.

B

Carved Koa Bracelet

ARTIST
Norm
Sartorius

MATERIALS

Koa wood, ¾ x 4 x 4 inches
  (19 x 102 x 102 mm)* (photo A)

Sandpaper: 120, 180, 220, 320, 400,
  and 600 grit

Rubber or cork sanding block

Oil finish or water-resistant wipe-on
  polyurethane

Clean cotton rag

Steel wool, 0000 grade

Paste wax

Soft cloth

*Koa retains its color without darken-
ing from UV light or oxidation. Other
dense woods, such as maple, ebony,
and bloodwood, would make hand-
some bracelets, too. Blanks for
bracelets are available from several
suppliers.

TOOLS

C-clamps or bar clamps

Drill press

2½- or 2⅝ inch (64 or 67 mm) hole
  saw or multispur bit

Band saw, scroll saw, or coping saw

Vise

Pneumatic sander (24-grit sleeve) or
  coarse wood rasp

Belt sander with 120-grit belt or
  wood files

Small, handheld rotary tool

Rotary cutter #115, ⁵⁄₁₆ inch (7.9 mm)

Small sanding drum for the drill press

Wood-burning tool

GROWN IN HAWAII, KOA'S SHIMMERING FIGURE, ITS VARIETY OF

COLORS, ITS HARDNESS AND TOUGHNESS COMBINE TO MAKE IT

A LUXURIOUS WOOD, PERFECT FOR A BRACELET LIKE THIS ONE.

Working Tip

Most bangle bracelets have
2½- or 2⅝-inch (64 or 67 mm)
holes. Check the diameter of a
bracelet that fits before you
drill your hole.

PROCESS

1. Secure the block of koa wood to the drill press with the C-clamps or bar clamps, placing a scrap piece of board or plywood under the block so you don't drill into the metal drill-press table. Use the hole saw or multispur drill bit to cut through the center of the block in one smooth pass.

2. Draw the rough form of the bracelet on the wood. Orient the notches on the long-grain sides (photo B). The bracelet is thinnest at these two places, so it should have the strength of long grain rather than end grain. Draw this form a little larger than the desired finished size.

3. With the bracelet blank held flat on the band-saw table, cut slightly outside your lines. Use a ⅜-inch (10 mm) blade or smaller to make these cuts, so that you can negotiate the tight curves. You can also use a scroll saw or a coping saw to make these cuts.

A

B

4. With the bracelet secured in the vise, use the rasps and files to refine and round the form. Work the form carefully until the blank resembles the form in the main project photo, minus the indented burned area (photo C).

5. The indented areas on the outside edge of the bracelet can be roughed out with a band saw. Make very short cuts close to but not at the final line for the depth of these notches. Using the small, handheld rotary tool and rotary cutter #115, or the rasp, carve these notches to their final depths.

6. After roughing out the notches, refine them with medium-cut wood files. At this stage you are refining the symmetry and creating smooth curving arcs on all the surfaces, as shown in photo C. Pay special attention to transition areas, such as where the tapered areas meet the thicker areas and the junctions between the bottoms and sides of the notches.

7. When the outer carved form suits your taste, you're ready to begin sanding the bracelet. The designer recommends using a rubber or cork sanding block. The block spreads your effort and helps prevent the rounded indentations that your fingers alone can make. Begin your sanding with 120 grit and progress to 320 grit. At each stage, you refine the form in small ways by eliminating facets or irregular curves.

8. Before progressing to 320-grit paper on the outer form, begin to sand the interior of the bracelet with coarse sand-paper. You can do this by hand, but a spindle sander will make this job go quickly. A small sanding drum chucked in a drill press will work as well. Moving the bracelet at all times ensures that the drum edges do not dig into the inside of the bracelet. Concentrate on creating a uniformly smooth surface. Move to finer grits (120, 150, 220, and 320) in succession. When you have smoothed the inside to your satisfaction, you are ready to finish sanding the outside form.

9. Return to the 220-grit paper, and break the edge where the just-sanded inside surface meets the outside form. Round the edge slightly to make this area friendlier to the wearer.

10. Continue sanding through 320, 400, and 600 grits. Be attentive to subtle changes in form, or even the occasional need to return to a coarser grit to correct an area you'd missed.

11. Check the notches for smooth contours and even arcs. They need not be sanded, but they do need to be accurate in form. Refine the forms, if necessary, with small files or sandpaper.

12. Clear your work area of sanding dust, sandpaper, and anything else that might burn. Plug in the wood-burning tool, and let it heat up.

It's a good idea to experiment on scrap wood prior to making the first mark on your bracelet. Push the tool against the scrap wood repeatedly to make a dark pattern. Once you're comfortable using the tool, burn the entire area inside the notches. Vary the pattern according to your taste (photo D).

13. Before applying the finish, inspect the sanded and burned surfaces of your bracelet one more time, and correct any mistakes you find. Then apply an oil finish as described on page 24 or a water-resistant wipe-on polyurethane, following the manufacturer's instructions.

C

D

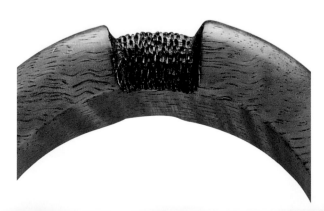

Holly Star Earrings

ARTIST

Judy Yunker, OSB

CHIP CARVING IS A CENTURIES-OLD NORTHERN EUROPEAN CARVING TECHNIQUE. THE GEOMETRIC BEAUTY OF A CHIP-CARVED SURFACE IS BOTH TIMELESS AND MODERN AT THE SAME TIME.

MATERIALS

Holly, ¼-inch (6 mm) thick and at least 1¼ x 3½ inches (32 x 89 mm)*

Cherry, ⅛ inch (3 mm) thick and at least 1¼ x 3½ inches (32 x 89 mm)

Sandpaper: 120 and 220 grit

Wood glue

Shop rag or paper towels

Tracing paper

Soft eraser or acetone

Oil finish

Cotton rags

Steel wool, 0000 grade

Cyanoacrylate glue

2 sterling silver eye screws

6 stone, wooden, or glass beads

2 sterling silver eye pins, 1½ inches (38 mm)

2 sterling silver French ear wires

Any light-colored wood with very little grain can be used to chip carve earrings. In this case, the cherry substrate creates a gentle contrast.

TOOLS

Small steel ruler

4 small C-clamps or spring clamps

No. 2 lead pencil

Chip-carving knife (small blade)

Vise

Scroll saw, or coping saw with fine blade

Flexible shaft tool or small, handheld rotary tool

Drill bit, 0.94 mm

Round-nose pliers

Flat-nose pliers

PROCESS

1. Cut the holly to 1¼ x 3½ inches (31 x 89 mm) using the scroll saw or coping saw. Do the same with the cherry, making sure that the grain runs in the same direction in both pieces. The cherry will form a substrate for the holly (photo A).

2. Before gluing the two pieces together, make sure they're flat. If they're not, sand them by rubbing them on 120-grit sandpaper placed flat on the table. Then apply wood glue to both surfaces, spreading it thinly, and clamp the two pieces together with the C-clamps or spring clamps. Wipe off the excess glue all around the joint with a shop rag or paper towel. Let the glue cure for an hour or more, then sand the large surfaces with 120- and 220-grit sandpaper.

3. Using tracing paper, transfer a star pattern to the holly twice for the two earrings. Use a pencil and ruler to sharpen the lines, but draw lightly to avoid denting the wood (photo B).

4. Practice with the chip-carving knife on some holly scraps held in a vise. If you are a chip carver, you will feel the difference between the basswood you may be accustomed to and the harder holly. Make sure your knife is razor sharp.

Beginning chip carvers should practice by drawing a triangle on a piece of softer wood such as pine or basswood. Hold the wood in the vise. Rotate the knife to a 30° angle, and make a cut along one of the lines, angling it down toward the center of the triangle. Beginning at the end of your first cut, angle the knife toward the center and

A

B

make another cut. When you've made the third and final cut, the triangle of wood should pop out. Draw the star on the softer wood to practice the slender triangles that this pattern requires.

5. When you begin to carve the holly, you may have to go over the cuts several times before the waste triangle pops free. Clean the cuts with the point of your knife. Use a soft eraser or acetone to remove any remaining pencil marks.

6. When the carving is complete, use the coping saw or scroll saw to cut to the outside lines of the star (photo C). Use a small piece of 220-grit sandpaper wound around the steel ruler to sand the sawn edges. Round the star points slightly. Choose the top end of each star, and use the sandpaper to make a flat area on its top point for the eye screw.

7. This is a good time to apply finish to the holly stars, before it can run onto the beads and silver. The artist used oil finish, following the process described on page 24.

8. Use the 0.94 mm bit in the flexible shaft tool or in a small, handheld, rotary tool to drill holes for the eye screws.

9. Put a few drops of cyanoacrylate glue on the shank of each eye screw, and screw them in slowly. Turn each eye screw so that its edge, not the hole, faces the front.

10. Thread the beads onto the eye pins. Form eye loops close to the beads by using round-nose pliers. Then twist the wire with flat-nose pliers until both loops face the same direction.

11. Connect the eye loops to the eye screws and ear wires, and close the loops.

C

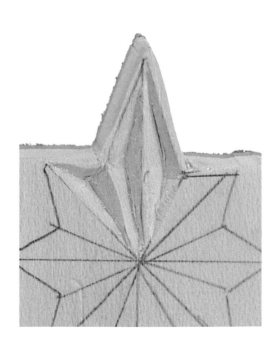

Floating Pearl Pendant

ARTIST

Aaron Barr

THE PEARL IS THE
STAR OF THE SHOW
AS IT FLOATS
MIDAIR, SIMPLY
FRAMED WITH THE
RICH TONES OF RED
AND BLACK.

MATERIALS

Ebony, ¼ x 1¼ inches square
(6 mm x 32 mm)*

Redheart, ⁵⁄₁₆ x ½ inch square
(8 mm x 13 mm)*

Aluminum oxide sandpaper: 150, 220,
320, and 400 grit (500, 800, and
1000 grits optional)

Sterling silver tubing, 3 mm outside
diameter

Epoxy, two-part five-minute

Paper towels

Plastic sheet

Oil finish

Cotton rags

Steel wool, 0000 grade

Paste wax

Sterling silver wire, 20 gauge

Freshwater white pearl, 5 mm,
half-drilled

Commercial sterling silver neckwire

Sterling silver wire, 14-gauge (optional)

*The square faces of the ebony and
redheart pieces must be long grain.
In other words, these pieces should
not be cut from the ends of square
pieces of wood (photo A).

TOOLS

Light-colored pencil

Compass or circle template

Drill, with ⅛-inch (3 mm) and
#65 drill bits

Jeweler's saw or scroll saw,
with blades

Half-round jeweler's file or full-size
round file

Drill press, with ¾-inch (19 mm)
Forstner bit (optional)

Small C-clamps (optional)

Coping saw (optional)

Vise or pliers

Scribe or nail

Narrow craft knife

Wire cutters

A

PROCESS

1. Use the light-colored pencil to mark the center point on the ebony.

2. Using the compass or circle template, draw two concentric circles around your marked center point, ¾ inch (19 mm) and 1 inch (25 mm) in diameter.

3. With the drill and ⅛-inch (3 mm) drill bit, drill a hole through the ebony anywhere inside the smaller circle.

4. Thread a saw blade through the hole, attach it to the jeweler's saw or scroll saw, and cut just inside the smaller circle (photo B).

5. Remove the saw blade, and use the half-round jeweler's file or full-size round file to remove any wood inside the smaller circle.

6. Using the jeweler's saw or coping saw, cut around the outer circle mark.

7. File and sand the outer surface to make a smooth circle. Try to keep the surface flat across and the edges crisp to make a nice joint with the redheart piece. If desired, you may bevel the inside edges of the ring slightly.

8. Use the pencil to draw the shape of the bail on your piece of redheart. Mark the top end of your bail. Using the ⅛-inch (3 mm) drill bit, drill a hole for the neckwire horizontally through the top end of the bail. Bore the hole while the bail piece is still rectangular and close to its final size. Hold the redheart in a vise or with pliers while you drill.

The designer created a softened, ⅜-inch-wide (10 mm) trapezoidal bail at the top, ¼ inch (6 mm) wide where it meets the ebony ring and about ⅜ inch (10 mm) tall. Decide whether you'd like the front of the bail to be completely even with the ebony or to be thicker at the very top. The back of the bail should be flat, flush with the back of the ring, but it can have a domed or flat front. Make sure that the grain runs horizontally, not vertically. You can sand away the excess when you're ready to attach the two woods (photo C).

9. Cut the redheart piece to size with the jeweler's or scroll saw. With the half-round or round file, curve the base of the bail so it fits tight against the ebony ring while the backs remain flush. Remember to site the bail on a long-grain portion of the ring. End grain doesn't glue well.

10. Now sand both pieces except where they'll join. Start with 150-grit sandpaper, and sand with increasing grits until you have achieved the finish you desire. For now, you can leave the bail a little thicker than the ring where they meet. You'll sand that area flush after gluing them together.

11. Push the 3 mm silver tubing through the hole in the bail. It should fit pretty snugly. Use the pencil to mark the tubing where it extends past each side of the bail. Remove the tube, and use your jeweler's saw to cut where you marked. File and sand the ends of the tube so they're flush with the sides of the bail. Use a scribe or a nail to roughen the outer surface of the tubing. This provides a better mechanical joint when you glue metal with epoxy.

12. Following the manufacturer's instructions, mix a small amount of epoxy. Spread a very small amount inside one end of the hole in the bail and around the end of the tube. Push the tubing into the hole. Immediately wipe off the excess epoxy with a paper towel. When the glue has cured, sand the bail sides and the ends of the tube if necessary.

13. Sand or file the two pieces of wood to make a tight joint. Spread out the plastic sheet on your work surface. Mix a little epoxy, spread it on both pieces, and press them together with their backs flat on the plastic sheet. Hold the pieces together for about five minutes, and then leave them undisturbed for at least 30 minutes while the glue cures.

14. Use the narrow craft knife to trim the excess glue. Sand any remaining glue away, and sand the front of the bail flush with the ebony. Again, use progressively finer grits to make the wood shine.

15. Apply an oil finish, as described on page 24.

16. Make sure that the 20-gauge sterling silver wire fits into the half-drilled pearl. Use the #65 bit to drill a hole in the very bottom of the pendant, opposite the bail.

17. Thread the wire through the hole you just drilled.

18. Use epoxy to glue the pearl on the end of the wire inside the ring. Clean up any excess glue right away.

19. After the glue cures, lower the silver wire to site the pearl in the center of the ring. Lower the pearl a tiny bit, and use wire cutters to trim the wire flush with the bottom of the ebony ring. Raise the pearl past the center, and fill the bottom of the hole with epoxy. Then push the pearl down until it's centered again. To hide the hole, mix some ebony dust into the epoxy, and press it into the hole. You'll have to work quickly.

20. Hang the pendant from a commercially made neckwire, or create your own neckwire with 14-gauge sterling silver wire.

B   C

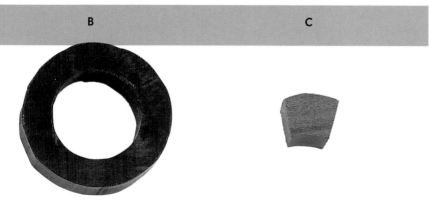

Lacewood & Silver Brooch

ARTIST

Hratch Babikian

DELICATELY GRAINED
LACEWOOD IS
GIVEN A SMALL, BUT
COLORFUL ACCENT
WITH A TURQUOISE
CABOCHON. CREATE
A UNIQUE SHAPE
FOR THE HANGING
SILVER ELEMENT BY
ADDING TEXTURE OR
PATINA TO IT.

MATERIALS

Lacewood (photo A on the next page), ½ inch (13 mm) thick

Drawing paper (optional)

Tracing paper

Cardboard

Dead soft sterling silver sheet, 20 gauge

Sandpaper: 120, 180, and 240 grit

Tie tacks

Turquoise cabochon, 6 mm

Rubber cement

Permanent marker, very fine tip

Sterling silver wire, 16 gauge

Earring posts and backs, silver or gold

Silver solder, medium or easy

Flux

Pickling solution

Cyanoacrylate glue or two-part five-minute epoxy

Shop rag or paper towel

Dowels in different diameters (optional)

Masking tape (optional)

Wet-or-dry sandpaper, 320 and 600 grit

Steel wool, 0000 grade (optional)

Green kitchen scrubbing pad (optional)

Oil finish

Cotton rags

TOOLS

Steel ruler, inch and millimeter

Pencil

Scissors

Fine-tipped permanent marker

Scratch awl

Jeweler's saw, and #2/0 with #8 blades

Band saw or coping saw (both optional)

Fine rasp

Flat or half-round files, 6 or 8 inches (15.2 or 20.3 cm), fine, medium, and coarse

Craft knife

Half-round, barrette, and fish-belly coarse and fine needle files, medium cut

Third hand

Soldering equipment

Flexible shaft tool

Cylindrical or oval burr, slightly small than cabochon diameter

Carving gouges (optional)

Drill with ¹⁄₁₆-inch (1.5 mm) drill bit

Round-nose pliers

Wire cutters

PROCESS

1. Draw your brooch designs—the carved wood and hanging silver shapes—on drawing paper, then trace the designs onto tracing paper (or just draw on the tracing paper). Transfer the designs to a piece of cardboard. Using scissors or a craft knife, cut out the shapes accurately to use as templates. Because the wooden part of the brooch has at least two levels, you'll need to make two or more templates for it, each showing a different contour.

2. Using a very fine-tipped permanent marker or a scratch awl, trace the shapes onto the lacewood and 20-gauge sterling silver sheet. Cutting just outside the traced lines, cut out the metal with the #2/0 blade in the jeweler's saw, and cut the wood with the thicker #8 blade (photo B). (You can cut the wood with a band saw or a coping saw if you like.)

3. Use the rasp and coarse files to reduce the wooden piece to your line.

Start carving the wood by knocking down the corners of the sharp edges, deciding where you want the surfaces to curve in or out. Animate flat planes by making them wave or twist; try to find how the shape wants to turn into a three-dimensional form.

4. When the forms are close to what you want, smooth and refine them with smaller, finer files and then with 120-grit sandpaper. After removing all tool marks with the 120-grit paper, remove the sanding scratches with 180-grit and 240-grit sandpaper.

5. Cut two ¼-inch (6 mm) squares from the silver sheet. Use the third hand to hold the tie tack pins while you solder one to each piece of silver. Place the squares on the back of the lacewood, and trace their positions with the scratch awl. Using a craft knife, carve out shallow depressions so the silver squares will rest flush with or slightly beneath the back surface.

6. Prepare a seat for the cabochon. You can do so using carving gouges alone, but a cylinder or oval burr on a flexible shaft tool will work more quickly. Choose a burr with a diameter slightly smaller than that of the cabochon, and make a hole half the depth of the stone. Glue the stone in place with cyanoacrylate glue or epoxy. Wipe away any excess glue with a shop rag or paper towel.

7. Shape the hanging silver part in the same way that you worked on the wood. Smooth the edges using medium files, then switch to fine files to finish smoothing and to remove any burr edges that have appeared. Using a light touch, curve the metal shape with your fingers. Slight curves often produce a big visual effect. Use dowels or other curved surfaces to help bend the metal evenly. If you must use pliers, pad the jaws with several layers of masking tape.

8. Drill a ¹⁄₁₆-inch (1.5 mm) hole close to the top end of the silver piece. Finish the

A

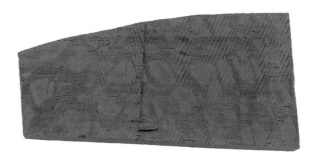

silver part by wet sanding the edges with 320- and 600-grit wet-or-dry sandpaper. Texture the faces of the silver with the 600-grit paper, 0000-grade steel wool, or a green kitchen scrubbing pad.

9. Drill a ¹⁄₁₆-inch (1.5 mm) hole, ¼ inch (6 mm) deep, at the center of the bottom edge of the wood piece. Use the round-nose pliers to make a tiny loop in the end of a piece of 16-gauge wire, slipping the silver piece into the loop before you close it. Use the wire cutters to cut the wire ¼ inch (6 mm) from the loop. Make sure that the pin fits into the hole properly; the loop should touch the wood. Put a little cyanoacrylate glue or epoxy into the hole, and dip the end of the wire into the glue before pushing the wire into the hole. Glue the tie tack backs in place, too. Wipe up any excess glue before it cures.

10. Use oil finish to darken and shine the lacewood. Follow the manufacturer's instructions or those on page 24.

B

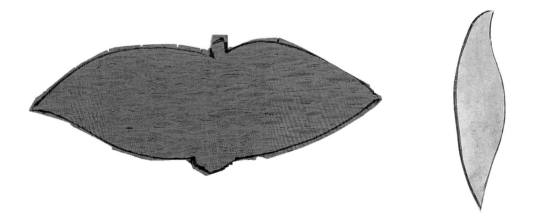

Segmented Twig Brooch

ARTIST

Joanna
Gollberg

THIS SLEEK BROOCH SEAMLESSLY MELDS SILVER AND WOOD.

YOUR CHOICE OF WOOD WILL MAKE IT A ONE-OF-A-KIND PIECE.

MATERIALS

White oak twig, approximately
⅜ inch (9 mm) in diameter*

Epoxy, two-part five-minute

Shop rag or paper towel

Sandpaper: 220 and 400 grit

Sterling silver sheets, 20 gauge
and 24 gauge

Hard silver solder

Flux

Pickling solution

Nickel-silver pin catch, joint, and
pin stem

Green kitchen scrubbing pad

*Any wood is suitable. Look for a
twig with a straight length suitable
for this project (photo A).*

TOOLS

Steel ruler, inch and millimeter

Jeweler's saw with blades

Flat file

Steel mandrel, 10 mm

Rawhide hammer

Soldering equipment

Flat-nose pliers

PROCESS

1. Find a twig about ⅜ inch (9 mm) in diameter, and peel off the bark. With the jeweler's saw, cut a straight length, 1⅝ inches (41 mm) long. File and sand the ends of the wood until they're smooth.

2. With the jeweler's saw, cut one round disc, the same diameter as the stick, from each of the 20-gauge and 24-gauge silver sheets (photo B).

3. Mark the stick at ⅜ inch (10 mm) and ⅝ inch (16 mm) from one end. Use the jeweler's saw to cut across the stick at the marks (photo C).

4. Mix a small batch of epoxy, and glue the 20-gauge disc and the 24-gauge disc between the sections of wood. You have reassembled the twig with two discs in it. Using a shop rag or paper towel, wipe up any stray glue, and let the glued twig cure completely.

5. With the jeweler's saw, cut a ¹³⁄₁₆ x 1⅝ inch (21 x 41 mm) rectangle of 24-gauge silver sheet. File the edges and sand them with 400-grit sandpaper.

A

B

C

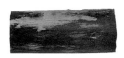

6. With your fingers, bend the rectangle over the 10 mm steel mandrel. The long edge should run along the length of the mandrel. Finish bending the rectangle into a perfect arc by hammering the metal over the mandrel with the rawhide hammer (photo D). Rest the mandrel on a smooth, firm surface such as a wooden stump or a secure tabletop.

7. Remove all scratches from the metal by sanding it with 220- and 400-grit sandpaper.

8. Solder the pin catch and joint onto the curved metal so that the center of the pin assembly is about 3 mm higher than the center of the curved silver (photo E). Pickle the piece and rinse it.

9. Remove any firescale by sanding with 400-grit sandpaper, and give the metal a final finish by rubbing it with a green kitchen scrubbing pad to create a matte look.

10. File off any excess silver from the discs in the stick. The silver should blend seamlessly with the wood. Sand the stick and the silver inlay to a 400-grit finish, but leave some natural wood grain showing for visual interest.

11. Mix some more epoxy and coat the inside of the curved silver section with it. Slide the twig into place inside the curved metal, and fill in any gaps with leftover epoxy. Let the epoxy cure.

12. Use your flat-nose pliers to attach the pin stem to the pin joint. If the pin stem is too long for the brooch, snip off the excess length, file the end to a sharp point, and sand the filed area to a 400-grit finish.

D

E

Carved Bead Necklace

ARTIST
Marjorie Schick

HAND-CARVED AND PAINTED BEADS
MAKE THIS NECKLACE A SINGULAR
PIECE OF WEARABLE ART. CREATE
AS MANY OR AS FEW BEADS AS
YOU NEED TO CREATE YOUR OWN
PERSONAL STATEMENT.

MATERIALS

Predrilled hardwood beads, 1 inch
(25 mm) in diameter*

Predrilled hardwood beads, 1½ inches
(38 mm) in diameter*

Hardwood cubes, 1½ inches (38 mm)
on each edge*

Hardwood discs, ⅛ inch (3 mm) thick
and ¾ inch (19 mm) in diameter*

Sandpaper, 220 grit

Wood putty or wood filler

Acrylic paint

Nylon rope, ³⁄₁₆ inch (48 mm) in
diameter

Paste wax

Soft cloth

Nylon upholstery thread

Clear acrylic gel medium (optional)

Dowel or paper tube (optional)

Paper cup (optional)

*The hardwood components of this
necklace can be purchased at your
local craft store.

TOOLS

4-inch (10.2 cm) C–clamp

Vise

Kevlar gloves

Goggles

Dust mask

Wheel and round burrs

Flexible shaft tool or small, handheld
rotary tool

Drill with ¼-inch (6 mm) drill bit

Drill press (optional)

Bar clamp (optional)

Center punch

Scissors

Upholstery needle

Small paintbrushes

PROCESS

1. To carve each predrilled bead safely, tighten the 4-inch (10.2 cm) C-clamp against the flat spots around the hole openings. Go one step further by holding the clamp in a vise so that you can use both hands for carving. If you hold the C-clamp in one hand, move it as far as possible from the carving wheel. Wearing a Kevlar glove is a good idea, as well.

2. Put on your goggles and dust mask. Using the wheel and round burrs with the flexible shaft tool or small, handheld rotary tool, carve some or all of the beads. Experiment with various shapes of burrs before making the final beads. The burr should feel as if it's digging into the wood slightly as you move it. If it wants to skitter away, move it in the opposite direction.

3. When the carving is finished, lightly sand each bead to remove any stray fibers (photo A).

A   B

4. Use wood putty or wood filler to repair any imperfections, and sand again.

5. Drill a ¼-inch (6 mm) hole through the middle of each wooden cube, using a handheld drill or drill press. Clamp the cube in a vise if you're using a hand drill, or with a bar clamp if you're using a drill press. (Hold the clamp instead of the cube while you drill.) Carve some of the cubic beads if you wish.

6. Separate the beads in your necklace with the manufactured hardwood discs. Mark the center of each one with a center punch, and drill a ¼-inch (6 mm) hole in each. Sand the discs for painting.

7. Paint your designs on the beads, cubes, and discs with acrylic paint. You can also paint the length of nylon rope to match the colors of the beads. After the paint has dried at least 24 hours, apply paste wax to both sides of the spacer beads to prevent the acrylic paint from rubbing off between the beads.

8. String the beads, cubes, and discs onto the nylon rope, adjust the rope length, and tie its ends securely. Add one or more beads to each end, if you wish, and knot the ends. Use nylon upholstery thread to sew the knots to keep them from coming loose.

Faux Carved Beads

An alternative way to create beads that look like carved beads is to buy a clear acrylic gel medium that is runny and has a stringy consistency. Place the bead on a dowel or paper tube to hold it, then drip the gel medium onto the bead to create the desired design. Place the dowel over something such as a paper cup that will support it while the bead on it dries. The wet medium will continue to drip, so the dowel must be rotated periodically until the medium is dry. The raised gel relief mimics the look of carved surfaces (photo B).

When the medium is dry, paint the bead as desired.

Window Treasure Pendant

ARTIST

Daniel Essig

ENSHRINE A TINY PERSONAL TREASURE IN THIS STRIKING PENDANT—

A FOSSIL, WISP OF A FEATHER, OR WHATEVER YOU FANCY.

MATERIALS

Mahogany, cherry, or walnut wood,
⅜ inch (10 mm) thick

Small found objects

Sized paper

Weatherproof wood glue

Water-based milk paint, green
and black

Sandpaper, 220 grit

Steel wool, 0000 grade

Soft cloth and rag

Brown shoe polish

Epoxy, two-part five-minute

Eye hook

Jump ring

Mica

⅛-inch (3 mm) brass nails

Leather strip or cord

TOOLS

Steel ruler, inch and millimeter

Handsaw or band saw

Scissors

Flat file

Paintbrush

Pencil

Drill or flexible shaft tool

#40 and #60 drill bits

Jeweler's saw with #7 blades

Needle files

Chisel, ¼ inch (6 mm)

Awl

Needle-nose tweezers

Small ball-peen hammer

PROCESS

1. Gather a few small objects you might want to display in your pendant. The designer often uses natural objects, but anything you treasure will work if it's an appropriate size—less than ½ inch (13 mm) square and ¼ inch (6 mm) deep.

2. If you have access to prepainted scraps of wood, part of your work is already finished. If you need to purchase wood, buy a blank ⅜ inch (10 mm) thick. In either case, cut a 1½ inch (38 mm) square from your wood, using a hand-saw or band saw (photo A).

3. If you are using bare wood and wish to achieve a leathery texture on the front of the pendant, make the texture first. With scissors, cut a 2-inch (51 mm)

square of sized (moisture resistant) paper, such as a brown paper bag. Wrinkle the paper by wadding it into a tight ball. Flatten the paper, leaving a little texture. Apply a thin, even layer of weatherproof wood glue to the front face of the square of wood. Lay the paper on the glued surface of the wood, and apply light pressure with your fingers. Make sure that the paper is securely attached, but don't flatten too many of the wrinkles (photo B).

4. Let the glue dry overnight for best results. Impatient jewelers might proceed when the glue has turned an amber color. When the glue has cured, remove the excess paper with a flat file, working from the textured side. This also bevels the edges.

A	B

C   D   E

5. The designer paints only the front and back surfaces, but you can paint the sides, too. To obtain the surface shown, use water-based milk paint in black and green. Paint the black layer first, covering the wrinkled paper on the front and the bare wood on the back. When this layer is completely dry, paint a coat of green over it. Just this once, don't sand between coats.

6. When the second coat has dried, sand the painted surfaces with 220-grit sandpaper. Sanding through to the black paint is desirable, but sanding down to the paper is not. Burnish the front and back with 0000-grade steel wool to darken and polish the painted surfaces (photo C).

7. Using the flat file again, bevel the front edges. Draw light pencil lines on the front, ⅛ inch (3 mm) from the edges. File back to the lines. On the back, just soften the corners a little, using the file or sandpaper.

8. Draw a ½-inch (13 mm) square, centered on the front of the pendant. Using the #40 bit chucked in a hand drill or flexible shaft tool, drill a hole completely through the pendant, anywhere inside the small square.

9. Beginning at the hole, cut to the line using the jeweler's saw with the #7 blade to open the window. Using needle files, straighten the walls of the opening.

10. Flatten one corner with the frame to make attaching the eye hook easier and to give the pendant a little more dynamism. The flattened area should measure ¼ inch (6 mm) wide for the ⅜-inch (10 mm) depth of the pendant (photo D).

11. Smooth any rough edges with 220-grit sandpaper.

12. On the front surface, draw a pencil line 1/16 inch (1.6 mm) from each of the four sides of the opening. Use the ¼-inch (6 mm) chisel to score and remove the painted paper layer in the 1/16-inch (1.6 mm) band. This creates a shelf to support the front mica pane (photo D).

13. Repeat step 12 on the back, but remove a 1/32-inch (.8 mm) depth of wood.

14. To seal the paint and slightly darken the wood, use a soft cloth to apply a liberal coat of brown shoe polish to all surfaces. After several minutes, burnish the wax with a soft rag.

15. Drill a hole in the center of the flattened corner, using the #60 bit. Drop a tiny bit of two-part epoxy into the hole, and insert an eye hook. Make sure that the eye is parallel with the faces of the pendant. Attach a jump ring to the eye for a leather cord.

16. Use ordinary scissors to cut two panes of mica to fit the inset shelves, each approximately ⅝ inch (16 mm) square (photo E).

17. Starting on the back, set a mica window in place, and use an awl to pierce the mica very close to a corner. Use needle-nose tweezers to insert the ⅛-inch (3 mm) nail into the hole, and tap the nail home using the small ball-peen hammer. Repeat this process in the opposite corner and then in the other two corners. This order helps ensure that the window is positioned squarely in place.

18. Select the found object to display, and place it in the opening. Consider using a few very tiny objects together. Remember that the top pane of mica has to lie flat in place, so don't try to stuff in an object that's a hair too big.

19. Repeat step 17 to secure the front mica window.

20. Hang the pendant on a leather strip, cord, or neck wire, as desired.

Slingshot Set

ARTIST
Robb
Helmkamp

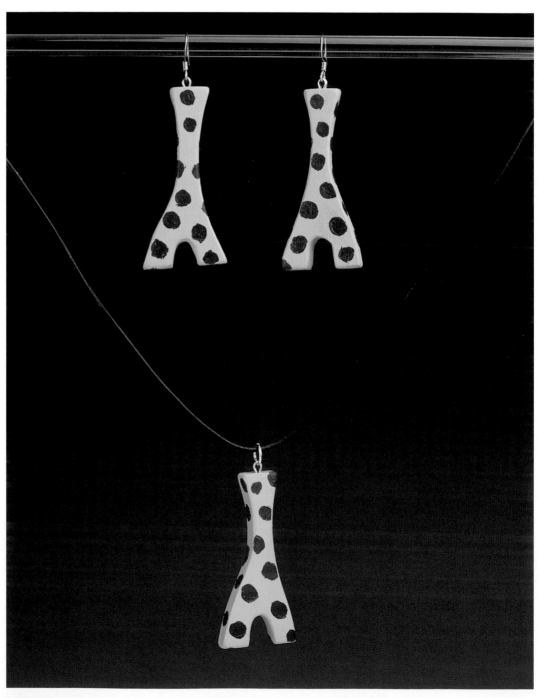

SLINGSHOT, SQUIG-

GLE, OR ELONGATED

OVAL—INDULGE

YOUR WHIMSICAL

SIDE BY CREATING

SIMPLE SHAPES OF

ANY SORT. WHAT

MAKES THESE PIECES

ESPECIALLY PLAYFUL IS

THE USE OF BRIGHT

COLORS PAIRED WITH

A SIMPLE PAINTING

TECHNIQUE.

MATERIALS

Poplar (photo A), ¼ x 1½ x 12 inches
(6 x 38 x 305 mm)

Sandpaper: 120, 220, and 320 grit

Brads, 1¼ inches (32 mm) long
(optional)

Acrylic paint, two colors

Epoxy, two-part five-minute

Eye screws

Shop rag or paper towel

Ear hooks

Jump ring

Black leather cord

Spring ends for cord

Clasp assembly

TOOLS

Steel ruler

Pencil

Fine-tipped permanent marker

Band saw or coping saw

Sanding block

Tack hammer (optional)

Drill with ¹⁄₁₆-inch (1.6 mm) drill bit

Small foam brush

Fine point bristle brush

Needle-nose pliers

PROCESS

1. With the pencil, draw lines across the piece of poplar, spacing them 2 inches (51 mm) apart. (You'll use these lines to limit the length of the slingshot shapes.) Then draw a number of slingshot shapes on the wood, keeping the long axis of each shape parallel to the wood grain. Choose the three that you like best, and darken their outlines with the fine-tipped permanent marker (photo B).

2. Using the band saw or coping saw, cut out the slingshot shapes, staying just outside the lines (photo C).

3. With 120-grit sandpaper, smooth the edges of the slingshots. Use the sanding block as much as you can, and roll up smaller pieces of sandpaper to smooth the tight concave sections. When you've removed all the saw marks from the edges, lay a sheet of 120-grit sandpaper paper on a flat surface, and rub the faces of the slingshots across the paper. Move with the grain, of course.

4. Use 220-grit sandpaper to remove all the scratches left by the 120-grit paper.

5. Drill a ¹⁄₁₆-inch (1.6 mm) hole, centered in the end of the "handle" section of each slingshot. Drill straight down the handle to a depth of about ⅜ inch (10 mm).

A

B

C

6. With the small foam brush, apply the first coat of background paint to each shape. The foam spreads the heavy-bodied acrylic evenly.

7. The first coat of paint raises fibers on the wood, so lightly sand those away with 320-grit sandpaper. Then add a second coat of paint in the same way you applied the first coat, and let it dry.

8. Use the fine, sharp-bristle brush to paint the polka dots or another motif. Mark the locations of the dots first by barely touching the surface with the brush. Then go back and press harder on the brush tip to paint full-size dots. When the first coat has dried, add a second coat with the same brush.

9. Mix a small amount of the epoxy thoroughly to make sure it will cure hard. Dip the threaded end of each eye screw in the epoxy, and twist it into the hole in a slingshot. Align the eye with the front of the slingshot. Before the epoxy begins to harden, wipe up any excess with a shop rag or paper towel.

10. Use the needle-nose pliers to open the bottom of each ear hook enough to thread it through an eye screw. Close the ear hooks with the pliers.

11. With the needle-nose pliers, attach a jump ring to the eye screw in the third slingshot.

12. Cut a length of black leather cord just long enough to position the slingshot where you want it. Pass the cord through the jump ring, and push each end into a spring end. Use the needle-nose pliers to crimp the spring ends tightly around the cord. Open the loop part of each spring end, and close it around one part of the clasp. Apply only enough force with the pliers to open and close the loop so you avoid breaking the wires.

Designer Tip

A drying board will make painting the slingshots much easier. To create one, find a scrap piece of wood or plywood, ⅜ or ½ inch (10 or 13 mm) thick. At intervals of 3 inches (76 mm) or so, drive 1¼ inch (32 mm) brads through the wood. Mount the slingshots by slipping the holes in their handles over the pointed ends of the brads.

Try other shapes to create variations of the slingshot set.

Topsy-Turvy Ring

ARTIST
Mayra
Orama Muniz

THE ASYMMETRICAL
CONSTRUCTION OF
THIS RING IS A
SURE-FIRE ATTEN-
TION GETTER.
THE CONTRAST OF
DARK EBONY WITH
ALUMINUM ONLY
ADDS TO ITS
ATTRACTIVENESS
ON YOUR HAND.

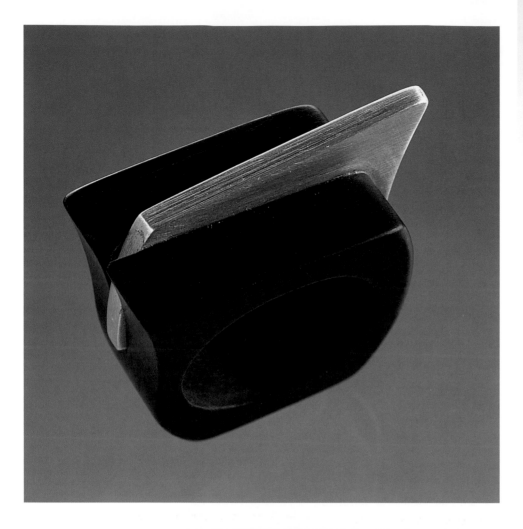

MATERIALS

Ebony, ⅝ x 2 x 1½ inches
(16 x 50 x 38 mm)

Aluminum sheet, ⅛ inch (3 mm) thick

Sandpaper; 120, 150, 220, and 320 grits

Epoxy, two-part five-minute

Oil finish

Cotton rags

Steel wool, 0000 grade

TOOLS*

Band saw, with one wood-cutting
blade and one metal-cutting blade
(optional)

C-clamp or small bar clamp

Drill press with ¾-inch (19 mm)
Forstner bit

Table saw

Handsaw

Coping saw or scroll saw

Sanding block

Bench belt sander with 120-, and
220-grit belts (optional

Scribe

Jeweler's saw

Metal files, flat and round

*This ring can be made with hand
tools alone, but two power tools—
the table saw and drill press—make
the work easier and more precise.
The instructions assume that you
have access to these machines.

PROCESS

1. Cut a piece of ebony ⅝ x 1⅜ x 1⅛ inches (16 x 34 x 28 mm) using any saw. The grain should run parallel to the bottom and top of the ring (photo A).

2. Secure a clamp to the ebony block, and hold the clamp while you use the ¾-inch (19 mm) Forstner bit in a drill press to bore the finger hole. Notice that the hole is slightly off center to allow for the asymmetrical shape of the ring.

3. Cut a slot halfway through the ebony using a table saw. This slot runs in the long-grain direction. Raise the saw blade to half the height of the ring, in this case, ¾ inch (19 mm). The saw blade should be ⅛ inch (3 mm) thick. Position the rip fence ¼ inch (6 mm) from the near side of the teeth to cut through the center of the ring's thickness. Place the ring blank on the table with the long, broad face against the fence and its narrow face down. Use a scrap piece of wood at least 12 inches (30.5 cm) long to push the ring past the blade. Hold the scrap with both hands, and push down and toward the fence with the extended index finger of your forward hand. As soon as the ring blank is completely clear of the blade, stop pushing, and use your forward hand to take the blank off the table. Don't let go of the scrap until you pull it backward away from the blade, still against the fence. If you aren't comfortable with this procedure, get help from someone who is.

4. Sketch a suitable shape for the ring, then cut it out with a coping saw, scroll saw, or band saw. The distinctive look of this ring depends on its asymmetrical shape (photo B).

5. If you have a bench belt sander, sand the edges of the ring with the 120- and 220-grit belts. Otherwise, sand the ring with successive grits of sandpaper wrapped around a sanding block. For better control, lay the sandpaper flat on the table, and move the ring over it. In either case, end with 320-grit paper. Keep the corners of the ebony sharp until the very end of the sanding process. Then round them only slightly so they maintain the crisp shape you drew in the first place.

6. Place the aluminum sheet in the slot in the wood piece, then use the scribe to trace the shape of the wooden ring, inside and out. Turn the aluminum and return it to the slot to show the ring's final appearance. You may find that you need to move the top line a little farther from the straight edge of the aluminum.

7. Use the jeweler's saw to cut this shape out of the aluminum. You will flip the aluminum piece lengthwise before gluing (photo C).

8. File and sand the outside edges of the aluminum until the curves are fair and smooth. Again, round the corners only a little bit.

9. Use epoxy to glue the aluminum part in place. Make sure that the aluminum leaves no gaps inside the finger hole.

10. After the glue has cured, file and sand the aluminum that still protrudes into the finger hole. Try to leave the ebony intact, working on the aluminum alone until it's flush with the wood.

11. Finish the ring with the oil finish, as described on page 24.

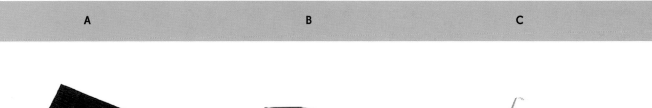

| A | B | C |

Slice of Nature Necklace

ARTIST
Vladimir
Levestam

ON YOUR NEXT

LEISURELY WALK IN

THE WOODS GATHER

MATERIALS FOR THIS

NECKLACE. WHERE

YOU LIVE AND WHAT

GROWS THERE WILL

ENSURE THAT YOUR

NECKLACE IS LIKE

NO OTHER.

MATERIALS

Dry wood twigs (oak, ash, plum), ⅝ to 1¼ inches (16 to 32 mm) in diameter, 8 to 10 inches (20 to 25 cm) long

Sandpaper: 320 and 600 grit

Natural wax polish (50 per cent organic beeswax, 50 percent oil of turpentine)

Soft cloth

Towel or cloth

Suede cord, 9 feet (2.7 m) long

2 cylindrical beads (photo A on next page), 8 to 10 mm diameter, 15 to 20 mm long, with 5-mm holes*

2 round beads, 5 mm diameter, with 2-mm holes

The designer used wood beads, but glass, ceramic, or metal beads would work nicely as well.

TOOLS

Steel ruler, inch and millimeter

Miter saw or table saw

Calipers

Vise

Drill, with 2- and 5-mm drill bits

Scissors

Table saw, miter saw, or handsaw

Pencil

Coping saw

Round file, ⁵⁄₁₆ inch (8 mm) diameter

PROCESS

Preparing the Strands of Wooden Discs

1. Collect some dry, straight twigs that have beautiful bark. To include slices of various colors in your necklace, choose trees of different species.

2. Cut the twigs on a miter saw or table saw into slices ³⁄₁₆ to ¼ inch (5 to 6 mm) thick. Use the calipers to measure their size. You should have at least 28 slices, ranging in size from ⅝ to 1¼ inches (16 to 32 mm) in diameter. Dry the slices in a dry, warm room for about one week. Save the biggest slice for a toggle clasp (photo B on the next page).

3. Sand the faces of the remaining 27 wooden slices with the 320-grit sandpaper. Lay the sandpaper on your work table, and move the slices across the grit. Then sand again with the 600-grit sandpaper. Don't sand the bark at all.

4. Make sure that your vise has soft-wood pads on its jaws. Grip each slice in the vise, and drill a 2-mm hole, from one edge all the way through to the opposite edge. Sight along the top edge to aim your drill bit.

5. Apply a coat of natural wax polish to the discs, and buff them with a soft cloth. Learn how to make your own polish on page 54.

6. On the cloth or towel, arrange the discs in three rows.

7. Cut a 24-inch (61 cm) length of suede cord, and tie a knot 6 inches (15 cm) away from its end. String the first disc, and push it against the knot. Tie another knot about ⅛ inch (3 mm) from the disc. Repeat the process until all of the discs in the first row have been strung. You should have about 6 inches (15 cm) of cord left at the end. String the other two rows in the same way.

Assembling the Necklace

8. Cut two 12-inch (30.5 cm) lengths of suede cord. Keep those and the two cylindrical beads close at hand. Arrange the three strings of discs parallel with each other and about ¾ inch (19 mm) apart. Gather the three cords at one end, and fold them back. The fold should be about 2 inches (51 mm) from the first knot. Make sure that each fold is as tight and flat as it can be. Slide about one-third of the length of a 12-inch (30.5 cm) cord through the folded loops. Fold the new cord where it touches the loops.

9. Pull the ends of the short cord through a cylindrical bead until it covers the joined loops. The suede cord should stretch enough to slide into the bead, and the bead should be tight enough to hold the cords without glue. Make the same joint at the other end of the strings of discs.

10. Using scissors, trim the ends of cord around the cylindrical beads to about ¼ inches (32 mm).

11. Fold one end of the necklace in half, and push a round bead over the fold. Pull the fold out of the bead to make a loop to go around the toggle.

Making the Toggle Clasp

12. Find the large slice, and draw a triangle with sides ½, 1, and 1⅝ inches (13, 25, and 41 mm) long. Cut out the triangle with the coping saw. Sand the triangular piece as before, but this time sand the edges and round the corners, too.

13. With the pencil, mark the centers of the two longest edges. Draw a light pencil line across the face of the triangle to help you sight from one mark to the other. Hold the triangle in the vise, and drill from one mark through to the mark on the other edge, using the 2-mm bit.

14. Using the ⁵⁄₁₆-inch (8 mm) round file, make a U-shaped groove across the longest edge of the toggle at the hole. The hole should be at the bottom of the groove. Sand the groove with 320-grit and 600-grit sandpaper. Finish the toggle with natural wax polish.

15. Push the remaining loose end of the necklace through the hole in the toggle so it emerges from the groove. String the second round bead on the cord, and push the end back through the toggle. Pull the doubled cord to seat the bead in the groove. Now the length of the necklace can be adjusted at both ends.

Silver Earrings with Epoxy Resin & Wood Inlay

ARTIST
Molly Dingledine

WHERE'S THE WOOD? IT'S CLEVERLY RECYCLED SAWDUST SUSPENDED IN EPOXY RESIN. WASTE NOT, WANT NOT.

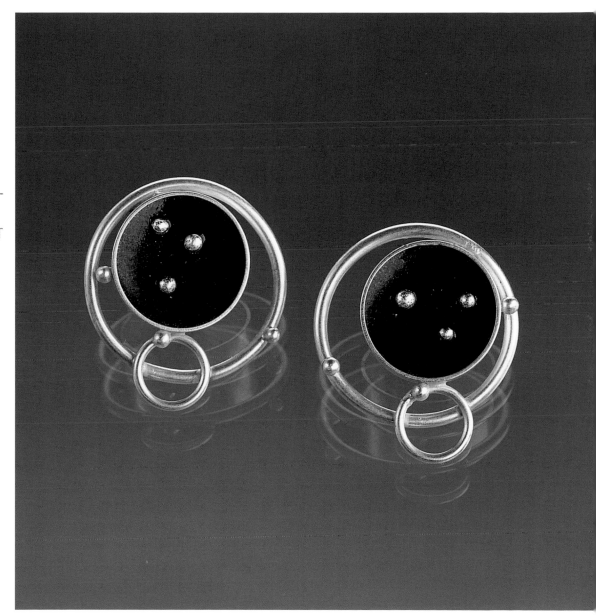

MATERIALS

African Blackwood sawdust (photo A)*

Sterling silver tubing; ⅛, ¼, and ½ inch (3, 6, and 13 mm) in diameter

Sandpaper, 220 and 400 grit

Sterling silver wire, 16 gauge (optional)

Sterling silver wire, 19 gauge

Fine silver wire, 20 gauge (optional)

Duct tape

Two-part clear epoxy

Disposable plastic bag

Other wood species work for this project, too. Just pick wood dust with a distinctive color. Collecting sawdust is getting more difficult because most shops have good vacuum systems. To make your own, first put on your respirator and safety glasses. Then crosscut a plank of the desired species several times, using a miter saw or table saw. Cut across the plank so that each pass cuts no more than the blade width. You'll produce nothing but sawdust. Consider any method that produces dust, not shavings. For instance, a belt sander with a 60-grit belt will produce plenty of dust for this project pretty quickly. A hole saw mounted in a drill press makes dust; so does a table saw.

TOOLS

Steel ruler, inch and millimeter

Template (optional)

Jeweler's saw with blades

Wire cutters

File

Round-nose pliers

Oxygen-acetylene troch

Third hand

Disposable syringe, tiny spoon, or toothpick

Needle

Flexible shaft tool and #61 drill bit

Tweezers

PROCESS

1. Begin by designing a pair of earrings, using sterling silver tubing and wire rings. You may use a template with various sizes of circles to help you design, or cut paper circles and play with possible designs.

2. Using the jeweler's saw, cut the silver tubing into slices, each ³⁄₁₆ inch (5 mm) thick. Once you have all of the pieces you need for your design, sand the rough edges with sandpaper. Begin with 220-grit sandpaper and then use 400-grit to achieve smooth edges.

3. If your design includes wire rings, cut the 16-gauge wire to the required length, and file or sand the ends to make them smooth before forming the ring (photo B).

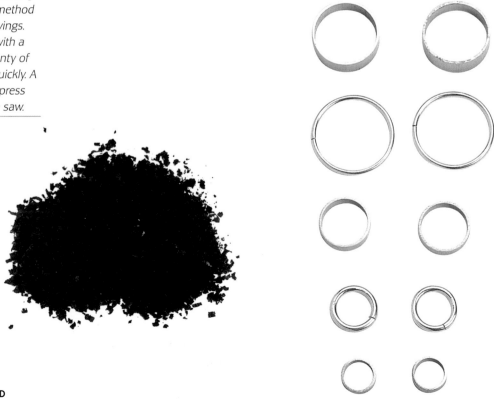

A

B

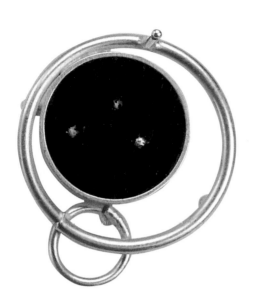

4. Use the 19-gauge wire to make two wire posts. File or sand the ends of the wires to make them smooth.

5. Apply flux to the pieces of tubing, then arrange them on the soldering block, according to your design, and solder them together. If you're using a piece of 16-gauge wire in your design, solder the pieces of tubing together first. After cleaning the soldered piece in the pickle, apply more flux and solder the 16 gauge wire.

6. To solder each ear wire onto a piece, place the soldered tubing on the block upside down, and place the ear wire in the third hand to stabilize it.

7. When the soldering is finished, clean up the joints with sandpaper and make sure the pieces are dry. Place a small

piece of duct tape on the back of any piece of tubing that you want to fill with resin. To prevent epoxy leaks, make sure the tape adheres to the metal.

8. Mix the two-part clear epoxy according to the manufacturer's directions. Mix the epoxy thoroughly for two minutes before adding any sawdust. Add and mix the sawdust a little at a time until you achieve the desired transparency (or opacity).

9. Lay a disposable plastic bag on your work surface, and prop up the earrings so that they're stable and the tube ends are horizontal. Using a disposable syringe or a tiny spoon (you can even use a toothpick), fill the pockets of tubing with epoxy resin. If you see air bubbles, gently blow across the epoxy until they surface, then use a needle to pop them.

10. After the epoxy has cured, peel the duct tape from the back. If you want granules set into the epoxy, cut small pieces of 20-gauge fine silver wire, each about ¼ inch (6 mm) long, and ball up the ends to make tiny pins . Use the #61 drill bit and flexible shaft machine to drill holes into the epoxy wherever you want a granule, but be careful not to drill all the way through. Push the pins into the holes to make sure that the ball ends sit on top of the epoxy. Mix a small amount epoxy. Using tweezers to hold the ball end, dip just the tip of a pin into the epoxy, and insert the pin into a drilled hole. Repeat with the other pins. Let the epoxy set, then enjoy wearing your new earrings.

Ebony & Silver Pendant

ARTIST
Bronwynn
Lusted

EBONY IS THE PERFECT WOOD FOR INLAYING SILVER, GOLD, OR BRASS. THE CONTRAST OF DARK COLOR AND METAL CAN BE AS SUBTLE OR DRAMATIC AS YOU DESIRE.

MATERIALS

Heavy paper

Ebony wood (photo A), ⅝ inch x 1⅜ inches x 2 inches (16 x 35 x 51 mm)

Sandpaper: 100, 220, 320, and 600 grits

Masking tape

Half-hard sterling silver wire, 1.2 mm and 0.8 mm diameter, each 15 cm long

Cyanoacrylate glue or epoxy, two-part five-minute

Oil finish (optional)

Cotton rags (optional)

Steel wool, 0000 grade (optional)

Carnauba wax flakes (optional)

Black PVC rubber cord, ⅛-inch (3 mm) diameter, 20 inches (508 mm) long

2 silver tubular end caps to fit 3 mm rubber cord

Paper towels or tissue

2 silver jump rings

1 silver clasp

Sheet of glass or fiberboard

TOOLS

Steel ruler, inch and millimeter

Black and white pencils

Pencil compass

Scissors

Awl

Band saw or coping saw

Drill press or hand drill

Drill bits: 4, 1.2, and 0.8 mm

Round file, 3 mm

Jeweler's saw (optional)

Rasp

File

Wire cutters

Tweezers

Small, handheld rotary tool

Sanding disc for rotary tool, 60 grit

Ball-shape burr, 8 mm

Small ceramic cup or bowl (optional)

Firm bristle brush for rotary tool, 22 mm diameter (optional)

Flat-nose pliers

A

PROCESS

1. On the sturdy paper, draw the side view of the pendant (photo B). The flat base is 2 inches (51 mm) long. Draw a light construction line ⅝ inch (16 mm) above the first and parallel to it. Using a pencil compass, draw an arc that connects the ends of the first line and just touches the height line. To position the hole, mark a point ⅝ inch (16 mm) from one end and ³⁄₁₆ inch (4.8 mm) above the base line. Cut out the template.

2. Using the white pencil and your template, trace the shape onto the wood. Use the band saw or coping saw to cut just outside the line.

3. Poke the awl through your template to mark the center of the hole for the cord on both sides of the ebony block. Using the 4-mm bit mounted in the drill press or hand drill, bore a hole through the ebony for the PVC rubber cord. Drill halfway through the ebony from each side to avoid tear-out and the possibility of drilling a crooked hole. Clean the hole with the 3 mm round file if necessary.

4. Draw the three slots on the top curved surface, and cut the slots with the band saw, coping saw, or jeweler's saw. The slots can be straight or slightly curved (photo C).

5. Use the rasp and file to shape and smooth the curved front. Don't get closer to the hole than 2 mm.

6. Tape a sheet of 100-grit sandpaper to a flat surface. Move the ebony to and fro on the sandpaper—always with the grain—to remove all the marks left from sawing. Sand all of the surfaces. When sanding the curved surface, start in the middle of the curve, and pull the piece toward you, turning it gradually to sand right up to the edge. This way, you're less likely to sand flat areas into the curve. Make sure that the various edges keep their right angles.

7. To sand inside the slots, fold a piece of sandpaper until it fits snugly in the slot. Pull the sandpaper through the slot, backwards and forwards.

8. Use the white pencil to mark the spots for the silver wire dots, and use the awl to make a dimple at each spot. Mark the larger holes. Using the 1.2- and 0.8-mm drill bits, drill all the marked holes 1/8 inch (3 mm) deep.

9. Use the wire cutters to cut enough ³⁄₁₆-inch (4.8 mm) lengths of 1.2-mm and 0.8-mm wire to fill the holes (photo D). Prepare a small amount of cyanoacrylate glue or epoxy. Pick up each piece of wire with the tweezers, dip it in the glue, and insert it into the same-size hole.

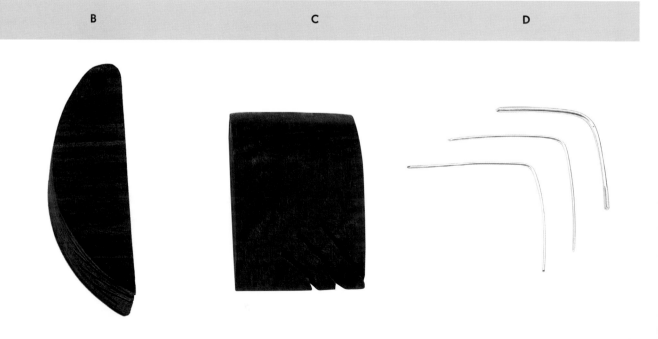

B   C   D

Ensure that the wire protrudes from the wood and that the glue fills the hole. You'll sand off any excess glue.

10. After the glue has cured, use the wire cutters to trim the wires close to the wood. Using the small, handheld rotary tool and 60-grit sanding disc, sand the silver and glue flush with the surface of the ebony. Try to avoid marring the wood surface. You can also use 60-grit sandpaper taped to the bench; this is the safest, but slowest sanding method.

11. When the silver wires are flush with the front surface and no glue remains, start sanding with 220-, 320-, and 600-grit papers, removing previous scratches with each grade. Remember that no finish can cover a careless sanding job.

12. To make the divots between the silver dots, use the side of the 8-mm ball-shape burr in the rotary tool. Practice first on a scrap of ebony.

13. You can use the oil finishing method described on page 24, or try soaking the piece in carnauba wax as the designer chose to do (see page 38).

14. Thread the pendant onto the PVC rubber cord, and adjust its length before trimming the ends with the scissors. Leave the pendant on the cord. Spread a little cyanoacrylate or epoxy glue on the ends of the rubber cord. Push the end caps firmly onto the cord ends, and wipe off any excess glue. Let the glue cure. Open two jump rings with the flat-nose pliers. Slide one jump ring through the end-cap loop that will be at the left-hand side of the necklace, and close the jump ring with the pliers. Catch the other end-cap loop and the clasp loop with the second jump ring, and squeeze the jump ring closed. This arrangement makes opening the clasp easy for a right-handed person. Reverse the sides if you're left-handed.

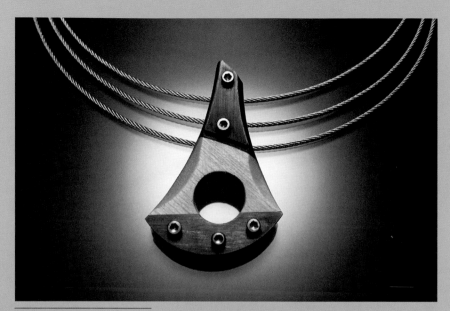

John Tzelepis
Untitled (#4 of 9), 2007
4.5 x 3 x 1.5 cm
Purpleheart, yellowheart,
brass, stainless steel
PHOTO BY ARTIST

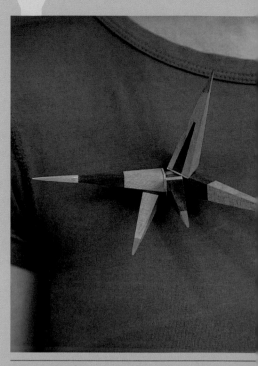

Cianán Doyle
Untitled, 2007
1.5 x 7.5 x 1.5 cm
Magnets, maple, teak, silver; hand fabricated, inl
PHOTO BY DEREK MCGARRY
COURTESY OF THE NATIONAL COLLEGE OF ART AN
DESIGN, IRELAND

Yuan-Fan Chen
Untitled, 2007
11 x 5 x 1 cm
Damascus steel, nickel alloy,
copper; hand fabricated,
metal-cut, manual saw, welded
PHOTO BY ARTIST

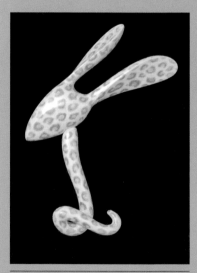

John Kent Garrott
Five Minute Burn, #1, 2005
11 x 11 x 2.5 cm
Wood, steel
PHOTO BY ARTIST

Bruce Metcalf
Jagrabbit, 2004
15.2 x 11.5 cm
Maple; carved, painted, drawn
PHOTO BY ARTIST
COURTESY OF CHARON KRANSEN
ARTS, NEW YORK CITY, NEW YORK

Michael Zobel
Ashanti Kingdom, 2003
1.5 x 5 cm
Ebony, 18-karat gold, black diamonds; fused
PHOTO BY FRED THOMAS

Anjanette M. Lemak Sidaway
hana-isho-marawu, 2005
2 x 20 x 22 cm
Mahogany, bronze, floral elements; hand-carved, cast
PHOTO BY ARTIST

Molly Dingledine
Carved Cocobolo Bracelet, 2005
4.5 x 7.5 x 2 cm
Cocobolo, cultured pearls; CAD, milled
PHOTO BY STEVE MANN

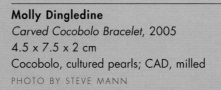

Mette T. Jensen
Ring (untitled), 2005
2.6 x 2.6 x 1.2 cm
Silver, beech; bent
PHOTO BY JOÎL DEGEN

Bronwynn Lusted
Mixed Bead Necklace , 2006
130 cm length
Average bead: 5 x 4 x 4 cm
Orange conkerberry, salvaged riverwood, brown mallee burl, mulga, orange box-wood, red mallee root, jarrah burl, tasmanian blackwood, padouk (wenge inner bead), blackbutt burl, red gum burl, huon pine, wenge, ebony, she oak, grass tree, myrtle, waxed linen thread; hand fabricated
PHOTO BY ARTIST

Carolyn A. Currin
Green Brooch, 2007
7.6 x 5.1 x 0.6 cm
Basswood, copper, acrylic paint; pyrography
PHOTO BY MARLENE TRUE
COLLECTION OF SHARON PERRY SULLIVAN

Francis Willemstijn
The Flying Dutchman, 2004
14 x 14 x 8 cm
Silver, ebony
PHOTO BY EDDO HARTMANN
PRIVATE COLLECTION

Liv Blåvarp
Prima Luna, 2005
28 cm length
Maple, whale tooth; dyed
PHOTO BY AUDBJØRN RØNNING

Joshua Salesin
Wave Bracelet, 2003
7.6 x 7.6 x 1.6 cm
African blackwood; hand-turned on lathe
PHOTO BY ARTIST

Kyoko Urino
Nature study series #1, 2001
40 cm length
Twigs, copper, patina; electroformed, hand tabricated

Nate Hansen
Honey Locus and Cedar, 2005
15 x 15 x 6 cm
Honey locus, cedar; turned

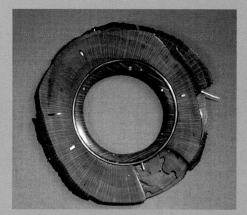

Jeannette Rein
Layers, 2004
13.5 x 13 x 1.8 cm
West Australian she oak, silver; riveted

Monique Escoulen
Untitled
7.5 x 5 x .8 cm
Horn slice, box wood,
leather; carved

Kirsten Bak
Unicated, 2006
3 x 4 x 4 cm
Wood, plastic

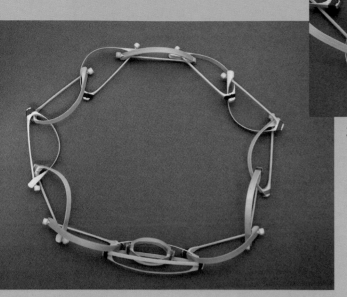

Walter Chen
Necklace, 2006
2.5 x 6 cm in diameter
Bamboo, nylon thread;
sharpened, tied
PHOTOS BY ARTIST

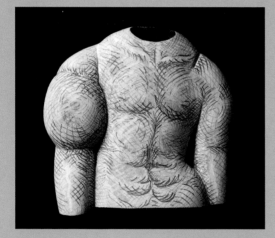

Catherine Truman
fugitive anatomie #2, 2005
7.5 x 7.5 x 1.3 cm
English lime wood, paint, Shu
Niku ink, graphite; hand-carved
PHOTO BY GRANT HANCOCK
COLLECTION OF ARTIST

Hratch Babikian
Purple Sail, 2001
17.8 x 7.6 cm
Purple heart, silver beads
PHOTO BY ARTIST

Bronwynn Lusted
*Riverwood and Conkerberry
Flower Ring*, 2007
4 x 5.5 x 5.5 cm
Salvaged riverwood,
Australian orange conker-
berry, sterling silver wire;
hand fabricated
PHOTOS BY ARTIST

Carolanne Patterson
Untitled (Brooch), 2006
14 x 8 x 3 cm
Wood, sterling silver, linen
PHOTO BY ARTIST

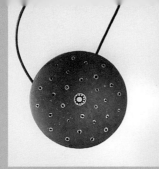

Ingeborg Vandamme
Necklace: Amulet, 1999
6 x 6 x 1.5 cm
Kneadable wood, brass, pigment, leather
PHOTOS BY RON ZÝLSTRA
PRIVATE COLLECTION

Michael Zobel
Timbuktu, 2003
2 x 2 cm
Ebony, gold, black diamonds; fused
PHOTO BY FRED THOMAS

Jim Norton
Untitled, 2004
7.5 x 3.5 x .75 cm
Copper, silver, dalmation jasper,
chopsticks; hand fabricated
PHOTO BY ARTIST

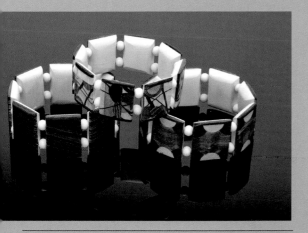

Robert J. Cutler
Linda Cutler
Untitled, 2007
2.54 x 20.3 x 0.6 cm
Bone, bacote, eucalyptus, holly, exotic wood, maple,
sycamore; laminated, inlaid, spalted, quilted
PHOTO BY KVITKA

Yu-Chun Chen
Untitled, 2006
18 cm diameter
Lime wood, silk thread, lacquer; hand-sawn, threaded
PHOTO BY ARTIST

Marjorie Schick
Red Square Brooch, 2005
7 x 5.5 x 1.9 cm
Wood, paint, stainless steel; constructed
PHOTO BY GARY POLLMILLER

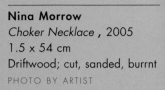

Nina Morrow
Choker Necklace , 2005
1.5 x 54 cm
Driftwood; cut, sanded, burrnt
PHOTO BY ARTIST

Yuan-Fan Chen
Untitled, 2007
7 x 5 x 1.5 cm
Ivory, rosewood, green sandalwood,
nickel alloy; hand fabricated, metal-
cut, manual saw, welded
PHOTO BY ARTIST

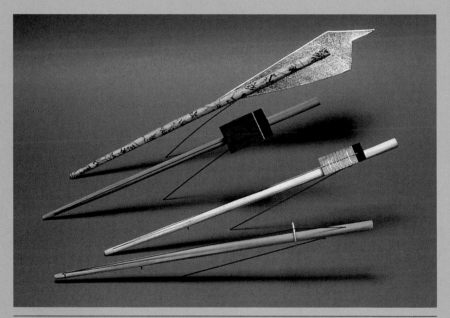

Robert Ebendorf
4 Brooches, 1999
16.5 cm length
Bamboo, silver, 24-karat gold foil, ebony, walnut, paint, string
PHOTO BY ARTIST

Kimberly Winkle
Mustard Faceted Bangle Bracelet, 2005
12.5 x 12.5 x 2 cm
Wood, paint, lacquer, graphite draw-
ing; faceted, painted
PHOTO BY JOHN LUCAS

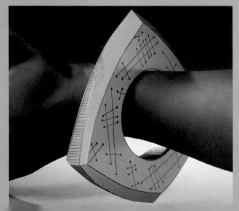

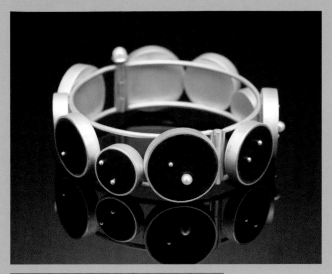

Molly Dingledine
Circles Bracelet, 2006
2 x 7 x 5 cm
African blackwood, sterling and fine silver,
cultured pearls; hand fabricated
PHOTO BY STEVE MANN

Bronwynn Lusted
Riverwood Ring , 2006
4 x 6 x 3 cm
Salvaged riverwood; hand fabricated
PHOTO BY MARK MCDACY

Mette Laier Henricksen
*Home Sweet Home, Cufflinks for the
DIY Man, Modern Style,* 2006
1.7 x 3.1 x 2.9 cm
Wooden panels, red paint, metal
PHOTO BY JEPPE SORENSEN

Daniel Essig
Epilegomena, 1999
10.2 x 7.6 x 3.8 cm
Wood, silver, brass, marbles, mica,
fossil shark teeth, Ethiopian binding
PHOTOS BY KEITH LOBUE

Liv Blåvarp
Spirits Talking, 2004
22 cm length
Birch, whale tooth; dyed
PHOTO BY ARTIST

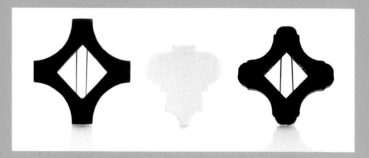

Mette Laier Henricksen
Home Sweet Home, 3 Brooches for the DIY Man, 2006
5.2 x 1 x 4.8 cm
Wooden panels, paint, sterling silver, steel
PHOTO BY JEPPE SORENSEN

Karrie Harbart
Ring Series #2, 2004
Left to Right: 2.5 x 3.2 x .6 cm, 3.2 x 3.2 x 1.3 cm,
2.5 x 2.5 x .6 cm
Walnut, paduak, purpleheart, model train grass,
epoxy; carved
PHOTO BY ARTIST

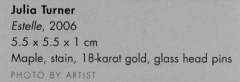

Julia Turner
Estelle, 2006
5.5 x 5.5 x 1 cm
Maple, stain, 18-karat gold, glass head pins
PHOTO BY ARTIST

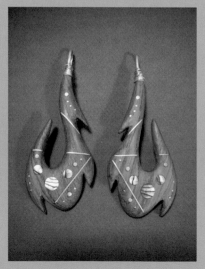

Tina Rath
Corallite I, 2006
5.7 x 4.5 x 2.5 cm
African blackwood, mink,
18-karat gold
PHOTOS BY ROBERT DIAMANTE
PRIVATE COLLECTION

Cara Leigh Sammons
Hei-Matau Earrings No. 2, 2006
9.6 x 4 x 9 cm
Teak, shell, nickel, silver; inlaid
PHOTO BY ARTIST

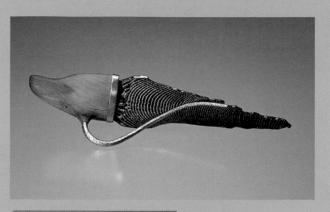

Harold O'Connor
Untitled, 2001
1 x 2.5 x 8 cm
Silver, 18-karat, applewood;
carved, cast, forged, fabricated
PHOTO BY ARTIST

Fabrizio Tridenti
Metamorphosis , 2007
9 x 4 x 1 cm
Aluminum, plywood, horn, color
PHOTO BY ARTIST

Francis Willemstijn
Grief, 2006
8 x 6 x 3 cm
Rosewood, silver
PHOTO BY ARTIST
PRIVATE COLLECTION

Kimberly Winkle
Faceted Bangle Bracelets, Group, 2005
12.5 x 12.5 x 2 cm
Wood, paint, lacquer, graphite drawing;
faceted, painted
PHOTO BY JOHN LUCAS

Elizabeth Rose Ditter
Root Series II #1, 2006
101.6 x 86.4 x 53.3 cm
Copper, rose roots
PHOTO BY ROBLY GLOVER

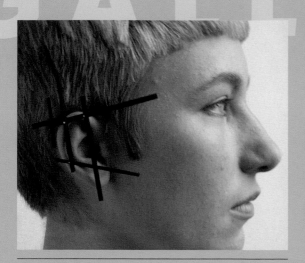

Franziska Kugler
Untitled, 2006
10 x 10 x 2 cm
Wenge wood, silver; riveted
PHOTO BY JOHN WEHRENS

Tina Rath
Boulder Colony, 2006
5.6 x 4.8 x .3 cm
Pink ivory wood, mink, peridot,
18-karat gold
PHOTO BY ROBERT DIAMANTE
PRIVATE COLLECTION

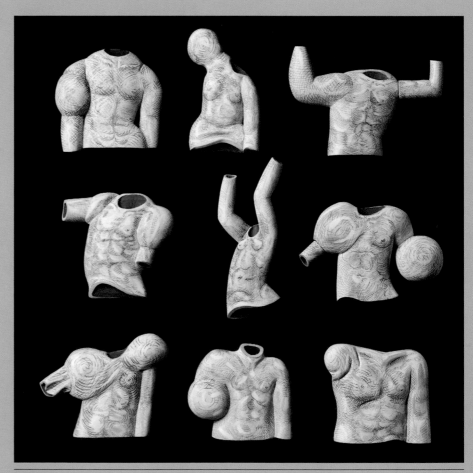

Catherine Truman
fugitive anatomies, 2006
12 x 12 cm, variable
English lime wood, paint, Shu Niku ink, graphite; hand-carved
PHOTO BY GRANT HANCOCK
COLLECTION OF ARTIST

Paul McEwan
White Root Ball, 2007
6 x 8 x 8 cm
Root ball; hand fabricated
PHOTO BY ARTIST

Liv Blåvarp
Untitled Necklace, 2007
28 cm length
Maple, palisander, whale tooth; dyed

Marcia A. Macdonald
*Wilma and Betty would
wear this,* 2003
Chain: 55.9 cm long
Bauble: 3.8 x 3.8 cm
Wood, paint, sterling
silver; carved

Robert Ebendorf
Brooch, 2005
12.7 cm length
Wood, silver

Saskia Bostelmann
Untitled, 2007
11 x 9 x 4 cm
Wood cooking spoon, gold foil,
18-karat gold, leather; pierced,
cut, varnished, hammered

Emma Bulpit
Untitled, 2006
15 x 19 x 1.5 cm
She oak, sterling silver; inlaid,
forged, carved

Mike Ruta
Multiple Skateboards, 2005
2.5 x 1 x 2.5 cm
Used skateboards; lathe turned
PHOTO BY YEVGENIYA KAGANOVICH

Suzanne Esser
Necklace, Untitled, 2006
4 x 21.5 x .25 cm
Birch, plywood, paint, black cord; laser technique
PHOTO BY MARTE VISSER

Mette T. Jensen
Bracelet (untitled), 2006
9.5 x 9.5 x 2 cm
Silver, beech; bent, laser cut
PHOTO BY JOÎL DEGEN

Molly Dingledine
Circles Brooch, 2006
40 x 40 x 10 cm
African blackwood, sterling and fine silver, cultured pearls; hand fabricated
PHOTO BY STEVE MANN

Linda Radcliff Sinco
Passage Bracelet, 2006
19 x 21.5 x 2 cm
Bamboo, sterling silver; oxidized, cold joined, fabricated
PHOTO BY REBECCA BARTON

Mette Laier Henricksen
Home Sweet Home, Cufflinks for the DIY Man, Classic Style, 2006
1.9 x 3.1 x 2.9 cm
Wooden panels, white paint, metal
PHOTO BY JEPPE SORENSEN

Mike Ruta
Skateboard Bangles, 2007
8.3 x 1 x 8.3 cm
New skateboard
PHOTO BY ARTIST

Rone Prinz
Heart on a Limb, 2002
3 x 2 x 1 cm
Sterling silver, bloodwood, deer antler, ebony, opal, amethyst, ruby, tourmaline, garnet; fabricated, carved
PHOTO BY BERNARD WOLF

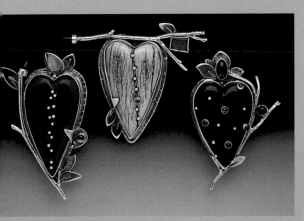

Walter Chen
Bracelet, 2006
2.5 x 10 cm in diameter
Bamboo, nylon thread; sharpened, tied
PHOTOS BY ARTIST

Ingeborg Vandamme
Necklace Wood and Silver, 2002
25 cm length
Silver, wood veneer; cast
PHOTO BY ARTIST
PRIVATE COLLECTION

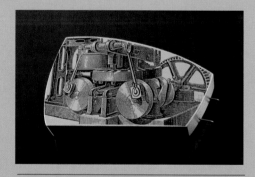

Gary Schott
Mechanism Brooch , 2006
9 x 5 x 2 cm
Basswood, acryclic paint, polyurethane, printed decal, steel wire; pierced, glued, sanded, painted, sealed
PHOTO BY ARTIST

Beate Klockmann
Bracelet, Untitled, 2005
10 x 4 cm
Ebony, 14-karat gold
PHOTO BY ARTIST
COURTESY OF GALLERY
MARZEE, THE NETHERLANDS

Martha Collins
L to R:
Helical Mosaic Chevron Bracelet, Brilliant Series
Weaver Bracelet, Brilliant Series
Linear Mosaic Bracelet, Straight Stack
All: 2006
All: 9 x 9 x1.5 cm
Exotic woods, cocobolo, ebony, maple veneer; dyed, laminated, turned
PHOTO BY STEVE MELTZER

Beate Klockmann
Chessnecklace, 2004
45 x 30 x 4 cm
Wood, 18-karat gold, chessmen; cut, reassembled
PHOTO BY ARTIST

Heather Beck
Honey Bee Brooches , 2006
64 x 64 x 9 cm
Mahogany, kingwood, brass rivets, copper, steel, water-based ink; three-layer silkscreen, riveted, chemically bonded
PHOTO BY ARTIST

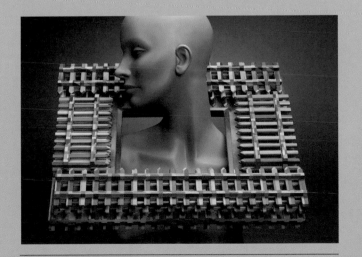

Marjorie Schick
Fences Necklace, 2004
45.7 x 45.7 x 7.6 cm
Wood, paint; constructed
PHOTO BY GARY POLLMILLER

Nina Morrow
Spindle Necklace , 2006
1.8 x 57 cm
Driftwood, cord; cut, sanded, dyed

Jeannette Rein
Slivers of Silver, 2006
36 x 3.2 cm
Jarrah, silver, ebony; laminated, riveted

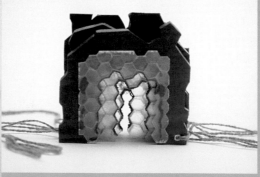

Seth Papac
entry, 2007
9 x 5.5 x 9 cm
Poplar, graphite, fiberglass, aluminum, enamel,
sterling silver, silk; hand fabricated, riveted

ABOUT THE ARTISTS

Hratch Babikian was born in Beirut, Lebanon, to a family of goldsmiths, watch-repairers, painters, and craftsmen. He came to the United States in 1979 and attended the Philadelphia College Of Art at University of the Arts, eventually earning his BFA in metals with a minor in photography. Over the past 12 years, he has been developing his oceanic series in jewelry and sculptural forms. His work has been featured in several publications, including *The Art and Craft of Making Jewelry*, published by Lark in 2006, and *1,000 Rings*, published by Lark in 2004.

Aaron Barr, of Seattle, Washington, is a studio-trained platinum and goldsmith and a self-taught woodworker. Creating custom wedding rings and one-of-a-kind designs, Aaron crafts pieces that are stylish, unique, and of the highest quality. His work can be found in art and jewelry galleries nationwide as well as online at www.aaronbarr.com.

Carolyn A. Currin is currently finishing her Bachelor of Fine Arts degree in Metal Design at East Carolina University in Greenville, North Carolina. She says that she has specifically enjoyed learning enameling and experimenting with various mediums like pyrography. Upon graduating, she plans to pursue a career as a studio artist and continue making art.

After receiving her Baccalaureate degree in occupational therapy from Eastern Kentucky University, **Constance Daly** went on to earn her Master's degree in Health Science Management, only to return to her crafts roots and enroll in the professional crafts program at Haywood Community College in Clyde, North Carolina. Constance believes that artistic expression is a part of health and uses this approach in her professional and personal life. She is now serving in the United States Army Reserve as an occupational therapist and continues to pursue crafts.

Molly Dingledine creates jewelry not only to adorn the body, but also to express a deeper meaning. "My admiration and fascination of the natural world, and my connection to it, is what inspires me to create," she says. After graduating from the Savannah College of Art and Design in 2005, Dingledine made her home in Asheville, North Carolina. Having grown up by the ocean in South Carolina, and now living in the mountains of Western North Carolina, she is continually inspired by the natural forms that surround her.

Monique Escoulen, from Mayenne, France, worked with her father making and repairing furniture as a young adult. She went on to own a workshop with her husband, a woodturner, and began creating jewelry in 1999. Her work has been featured in galleries in France, as well as Philadelphia, Pennsylvania, and Weaverville, North Carolina.

Daniel Essig lives in Asheville, North Carolina, where he is a full-time studio artist specializing in the book arts. He earned a BA in Photography from Southern Illinois University at Carbondale. He received a North Carolina Visual Artist Fellowship in 2002 and regularly teaches classes at Penland School of Crafts, Arrowmont Craft School, and John C. Campbell Folk School.

Joanna Gollberg is a nationally recognized jeweler, metalsmith, teacher, and writer. Her works have won numerous awards, including one from the American Jewelry Design Council and Lapidary Journal. Joanna is the author of several books, including *Making Metal Jewelry*, *Creative Metal Crafts*, and *The Art & Craft of Making Jewelry*, all published by Lark Books.

Marcy Grant began her fixation on design at a young age. Her passion motivated her to study graphic, industrial and jewelry design at the University of Michigan in Ann Arbor. She moved to Chicago in 1998 and began to focus on the design of wearable art. She works out of her loft on Chicago Avenue and sells her work through shows, boutiques, by appointment, and through her web site, www.formoda.com.

Growing up all over the country and traveling overseas, **Robb Helmkamp** has been exposed to a wide variety of folk art traditions. Continually inspired by the raw feel, honesty, and rough beauty of folk art, he enjoys incorporating it into his woodworking, sculpture, and design. Kicking the utilitarian, mundane, and ordinary up a notch, he creates work that is whimsical, colorful, fun, and unique. A recent graduate of Haywood Community College, he displays his fly-swatters, sculpture, and furniture at various Western North Carolina galleries and exhibitions. Robb lives with his photo book-editing wife Kara, very smart dog Isis, and fat orange cat Odille in Asheville, North Carolina. His work can be seen online at www.rhelm-works.com

Georgie Anne Jaggers is a beaded jewelry and home accents artist in Asheville, North Carolina, where she manages Chevron Trading Post & Bead Co. Going into her fifth year of teaching, she's had her work featured in books, magazines, and on television. Beading is her passion and she wants to share it with everyone around her—friends, students, and customers. She is open to all beads, all color palates, and any style, from elegant to whimsical. Her work has appeared in *Beautiful Beaded Home* and *Bead Love*, published by Lark Books in 2006 and 2007, respectively.

Karen J. Lauseng is an accomplished metalsmith residing in Silver City, New Mexico. She received BFA and MFA degrees from Kansas State University.

Her artwork has been showcased in numerous magazines including *Art Jewelry, The Crafts Report* and *Creative Home Arts.* Her work has also been published in *The Art of Jewelry, Paper Jewelry* and *500 Earrings*, all published by Lark Books. Karen's jewelry designs can be seen at www.kjartworks.net.

Cyndi Lavin is a mixed media artist who lives, plays, and makes art in Ayer, Massachusetts. Cyndi's work and her articles appear regularly in wearable art magazines and books. Her work can be seen at www.mazeltovjewelry.com, and she also blogs on www.bead-arts.com and www.layersuponlayers.com, where she shares tips and tutorials, artist profiles, and lots of resources every weekday.

Vladimir Levestam, of Yalta, Ukraine, became interested in art while studying theoretical physics at Moscow State University and Simferopol State University. He worked as a designer for the Botanical Gardens in Yalta, where he became deeply involved in conceptual art, namely abstract and mechanical sculpture. Wood became his favorite medium. He received a Master of Decorative Arts degree from the Ukraine Artists' Union in 1985. He has exhibited work throughout Russia and the Ukraine, the United States, Germany, Japan, and France. He owns his own business, Loewestamm Wooden Jewelry, which can be found online at http://woodenjewellery.com. Levestam lives in Yalta with his third wife and three children.

Bronwynn Lusted and her husband, **Paul McEwan**, grew up in a small coastal town in eastern Australia and have been making wooden jewelry since early 2005. The beautiful range of Australian timbers available to the couple, whether found on a walk through the bush, submerged in a creek, or on the shelves of a timber shop, provide them with unlimited possibilities for a lifetime of creative jewelry making. Their designs can be seen online at www.banglesofwood.com.

Using exotic hardwoods as an expression of life in organic moving forms, **Mayra Orama Muniz** has created a line of jewelry that reflects her life growing up in New York City and the more recent influences of her last five years in Puerto Rico. The landscapes of her life, from the modern industrial city to the tropical rain forests of Puerto Rico, are her inspiration. The miniature sculptures she creates are a melding of richly textured woods and cool metals that hint at the natural flowing beauty of the lush green mountains of Utuado and the pristine white sand beaches of Vega Baja. An admirer of Henry Moore she is also influenced by Asian art, she is drawn to creating balance and movement in her work. Mayra is self-taught, and wishes to remain so.

Norm Sartorius of Parkersburg, WV, has been obsessed with wooden spoons throughout his 30-year career as a woodworker. He has spent the last 17 years exploring spoons as a context for sculpture. Each piece evolves as collaboration with wood and an exploration of his state of mind at the time. Norm exhibits at top national craft shows and has spoons in the collections of Museum of Art and Design in New York City, the Detroit Institute of Art, the Yale University Art Gallery, and the National Museum of American Art of the Smithsonian Institution. He also carves letter openers and wooden bracelets. His work can be seen at www.normsartorius.com.

Marjorie Schick is an internationally recognized artist whose work is featured in the permanent collections of such Institutions as the Victoria and Albert Museum in London, the Royal Museum of the National Museums of Scotland, and the National Museum of Modern Art in Kyoto, Japan. She received her undergraduate degree in Art Education from the University of Wisconsin-Madison, then studied under master jeweler Alma Eikerman at Indiana University, Bloomington, obtaining her MFA in 1966. Schick has been a faculty member at Pittsburg State University in Kansas since 1967. In recognition of her distinguished artistic career, she was named a Fellow of the American Craft Council in both 2000 and 2002, and also received the Kansas Governor's Artist Award. She also served as juror for *500 Necklaces*, published by Lark in 2006.

Cynthia B. Wuller received her BFA from the School of the Art Institute of Chicago. She currently creates jewelry, accessories, and clothing. Her love of shapes and textural contrasts shows in all her pieces. Her jewelry is featured in magazines and books including *The Art of Jewelry: Paper Jewelry* published by Lark in 2006.

Sister Judy Yunker began carving wood as an apprentice under Kentucky carver Roy May in 2000. While attending John C. Campbell Folk School in Brasstown, NC, on sabbatical in 2001, she studied chip carving under Red Rainey. The love of carving rubbed off on Judy, who began carving full time in 2005. She lives in eastern Kentucky and is active in the Kentucky Guild of Artists & Craftsmen, the David Appalachian Craft Center, and the Oil Springs Center for the Arts & Recreation.

Index